# GILLIAN CONAHAN

# *Handwear* HANDBOOK

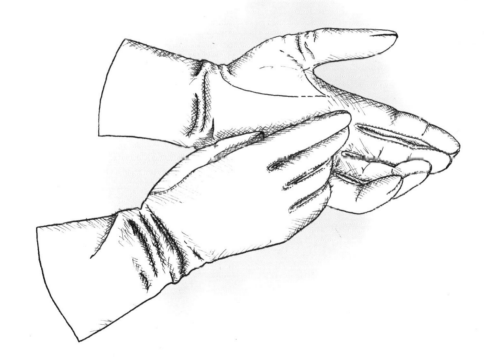

## MAKE GLOVES, CUFFS & VAMBRACES
### *for Cosplay & Beyond*

**FanP⚙weredPRESS**
*IMAGINE | MAKE | BECOME*

**PUBLISHER:** Amy Barrett-Daffin

**CREATIVE DIRECTOR:** Gailen Runge

**SENIOR EDITOR:** Roxane Cerda

**TECHNICAL EDITORS:** Kristyne Czepuryk and Debbie Rodgers

**COVER/BOOK DESIGNER:** April Mostek

**PRODUCTION COORDINATOR:** Zinnia Heinzmann

**ILLUSTRATORS:** Gillian Conahan and Mary Flynn

**PHOTOGRAPHY COORDINATOR:** Lauren Herberg

**PHOTOGRAPHY ASSISTANT:** Rachel Ackley

**FRONT COVER AND STYLED PHOTOGRAPHY** by Neil Bonabon (pages 3–6, 34, 38, 44, 50, 54, 58, 65–66, 68, 78, 84, and 90)

**HOW-TO PHOTOGRAPHY** by Gillian Conahan, unless otherwise noted

Published by FanPowered Press, an imprint of C&T Publishing, Inc., P.O. Box 1456, Lafayette, CA 94549

Attention Teachers: C&T Publishing, Inc., encourages the use of our books as texts for teaching. You can find lesson plans for many of our titles at ctpub.com or contact us at ctinfo@ctpub.com.

We take great care to ensure that the information included in our products is accurate and presented in good faith, but no warranty is provided, nor are results guaranteed. Having no control over the choices of materials or procedures used, neither the author nor C&T Publishing, Inc., shall have any liability to any person or entity with respect to any loss or damage caused directly or indirectly by the information contained in this book. For your convenience, we post an up-to-date listing of corrections on our website (ctpub.com). If a correction is not already noted, please contact our customer service department at ctinfo@ctpub.com or P.O. Box 1456, Lafayette, CA 94549.

Trademark (™) and registered trademark (®) names are used throughout this book. Rather than use the symbols with every occurrence of a trademark or registered trademark name, we are using the names only in the editorial fashion and to the benefit of the owner, with no intention of infringement.

Library of Congress Cataloging-in-Publication Data

Names: Conahan, Gillian, author.
Title: Handwear handbook : make gloves, cuffs & vambraces for cosplay & beyond / Gillian Conahan.
Description: Lafayette : FanPowered Press, [2023] | Summary: "Handwear Handbook guides readers through techniques and tips to create all forms of hand and arm-wear, from basic cuffs and bracers to gloves, armor, and more! This book covers every step of the process to simplify glove making and offer crafters a range of pieces that adapt to any style"-- Provided by publisher.
Identifiers: LCCN 2022041803 | ISBN 9781644032756 (trade paperback) | ISBN 9781644032763 (ebook)
Subjects: LCSH: Gloves. | Cuffs (Clothing) | Cosplay.
Classification: LCC TT666 .C66 2023 | DDC 646.4/8--dc23/eng/20220902
LC record available at https://lccn.loc.gov/2022041803

Printed in the USA

10 9 8 7 6 5 4 3 2 1

*To the Squirtle Squad*

## ACKNOWLEDGMENTS

I'm grateful to all the colleagues and fellow creatives who challenge me to be a better and more ambitious maker, but a few specifics deserve mention. Many thanks to Neil, whose sensible approach and impeccable eye made my project basket chaos into art. Lauren, peerless photoshoot buddy and painting consultant, your skill and meticulousness continue to inspire. Thank you KT and Kathleen for focus grouping, moral support, and telling me the thumb piece is still backward. Thanks to Carly for aesthetic judgment and encouraging healthy coffee break habits, and to Goran for digging up the most remarkable specimens of handwear fashion. As ever, boundless gratitude to my eagle-eyed agent Andrea Somberg. And, of course, thank you to Roxane and the fabulous C&T team for indulging my esoteric interest in handwear.

# CONTENTS

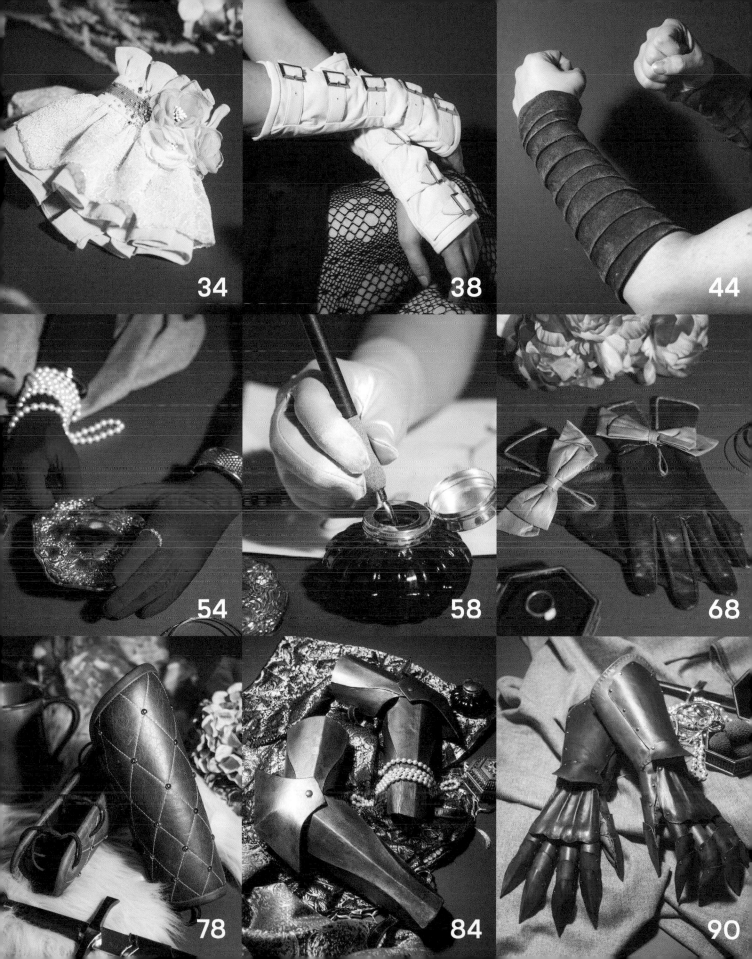

34

38

44

54

58

68

78

84

90

# WELCOME, GLOVE MAKERS

Hands are difficult to dress. They're small, complicated, extremely mobile, and their function must come before everything else. To get through a whole day in costume, you should be able to manage bags and props, scratch an itch, and send a text. Anything that limits essential functions takes you into advanced costume-wearing territory, the sort of thing that, ideally, happens for shorter periods of time or with a handler nearby to assist.

Given all this fussiness and inconvenience, gloves can hardly seem worth it when they are also notoriously tricky to sew. While this reputation may be a bit overblown, it's true that they use relatively tricky materials like leather and spandex, the pieces and seam allowances are tiny, and they're full of hairpin pivots that have to be executed with utmost precision. All of this takes practice and patience to overcome, but that just makes it more satisfying once you've accomplished it.

Despite all the obstacles, there are few things that complete a costume like a pair of gloves. For certain historical periods, they're essential, and few people from the period would have appeared in public without them. With a fully-armored suit, bare hands are blisteringly obvious and can look comically tiny. And gloves can also be adorable, elegant, stately, threatening, or sexy. So I propose to you that the fuss and effort are all worth it.

If you're still not convinced, relax. You can try your hand at some of the other armwear in this book, whether you lean toward lacy cuffs or rugged wraps. You can try out simplified gloves and proceed to the fully gusseted version once you've convinced yourself of the advantages. I'll make a glove maker of you yet.

## A GLOVE AND ARMOR GLOSSARY

The **TRANK** is the body of the glove, cut in one or two pieces to cover the palm, back of the hand, and fingers. Shapes may vary but the palm side will be shaped to accommodate the thumb. Most decorative detailing is concentrated on the back of the hand.

**GUSSETS** or **FOURCHETTES** (from the French word for *forks*) are used between the fingers because the trank alone doesn't usually allow enough material to wrap all the way around each finger. Unless the material is very stretchy, omitting gussets will result in gloves that are unwearably tight in the fingers, floppy and loose in the palm, or both.

Some historical or very fancy glove patterns use **QUIRKS** at the base of the fourchettes to allow extra room for movement. These tiny additional triangular or diamond-shaped gussets aren't required in all cases, but they can add interesting detail if you're inclined to be extra fancy.

Glove makers use different terms for several standard seam types. An **INSEAMED GLOVE** is sewn with right sides together and then turned right side out, like most other garments. A **PRIX SEAM** is sewn wrong sides together, with neat, narrow seam allowances exposed. A **PIQUE SEAM** is a lapped seam in which one edge is laid over the other and then they're stitched together down the middle.

INSEAMED

PIQUE SEAM

PRIX SEAM

Some fitted glove styles include a set of pintucks called **POINTS** to add shape and detail to the back of the hand.

The length of a glove is traditionally measured by the **BUTTON LENGTH**, which is the distance in inches from the base of the thumb to the hem but refers to the number of buttons needed to close the glove up the arm. Although not mandatory in the era of stretch fabrics and zippers, a button closure can still be a dramatic and elegant style detail.

**BRACERS** are short pieces of forearm armor, often associated with archers, that typically extend from the wrist to below the elbow.

A **GAUNTLET** is an armored glove, but the term can also refer to a large decorative cuff on a regular set of gloves, often heavily embroidered or trimmed.

**VAMBRACES** cover almost the entire arm and consist of upper and lower **CANNONS** (tubes) and a **COUTER** covering the elbow. These may be hinged together into one segmented unit, or they may be connected with flexible leather or fabric straps.

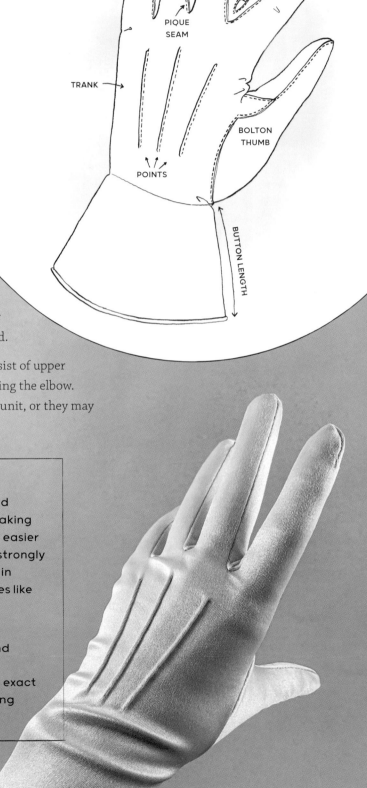

### A Note on Measurements

Although this book provides both imperial and metric measurements in most cases, glove making requires a high level of precision that is often easier to accomplish using metric measurements. I strongly suggest that you record your measurements in millimeters, especially for very small distances like the circumference of a finger.

The metric measurements in this book follow standard conversion practices for sewing and soft crafts. The metric equivalents are often rounded off for ease of use. If you need more exact measurements, there are a number of amazing online converters.

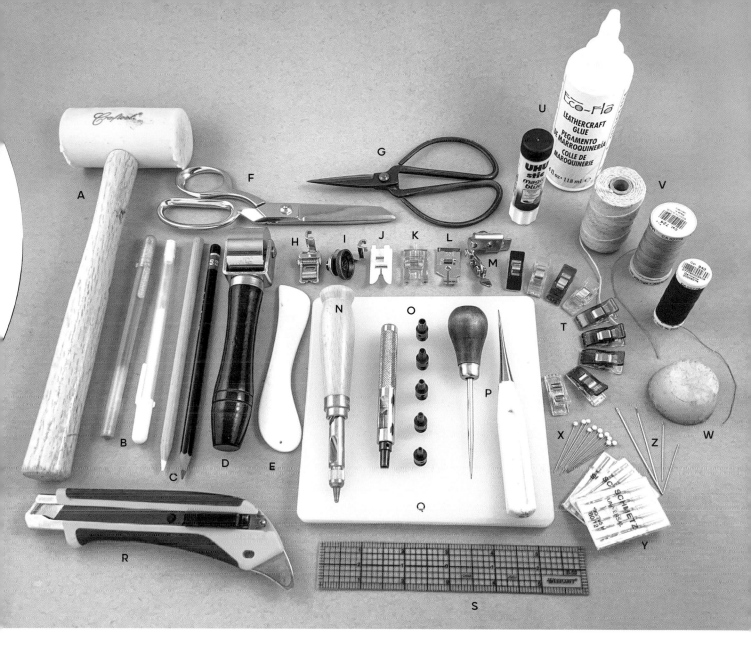

## SUPPLIES

**A:** Mallet

**B:** Gel pens

**C:** Chalk and soft graphite pencils

**D:** Seam roller

**E:** Bone folder

**F:** Fabric shears

**G:** Trimming scissors

**H:** Roller foot

**I:** Wheel-style roller foot

**J:** Nonstick foot

**K:** Clear foot

**L:** Straight stitch foot

**M:** Adjustable zipper foot

**N:** Screw punch

**O:** Drive punch

**P:** Awls

**Q:** Cutting board

**R:** Craft knife

**S:** Ruler

**T:** Fabric clips

**U:** Glues

**V:** Threads

**W:** Beeswax

**X:** Pins

**Y:** Machine-sewing needles

**Z:** Hand-sewing needles

**CARDSTOCK OR HEAVY PAPER** Copy your patterns onto heavyweight paper so you can easily trace them onto your fabric.

**MARKING TOOLS** You'll need an assortment of pens and pencils to mark clearly and accurately on different materials. A soft pencil or chalk pencil works on most fabrics, a white charcoal pencil makes clear marks that brush away easily, and a white or silver gel pen is great for leather. If you are marking on the fabric face, always test first to make sure the marks will remove cleanly when you're done.

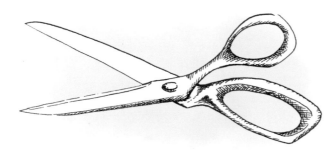

**FABRIC SHEARS** These should be very sharp. You can use them to cut things that aren't fabric if you desperately want to, but make friends with your local sharpener if you do. Otherwise, cherish and protect them with your life.

**TRIMMING SCISSORS** Similar to fabric shears, just smaller, trimming scissors should also be kept very sharp.

**CRAFT KNIFE AND CUTTING MAT** Some people prefer a knife for cutting clean lines and fine detail, especially on leather. Go for it, but be sensible and watch your fingers. Using a cutting mat helps you get a clean cut and keeps your blades fresh longer.

**PINS** I like silk pins for lightweight materials and detailed projects.

**FABRIC CLIPS** Clips are a popular pin alternative for leather and for sewing in general. Feel free to substitute mini binder clips or paper clips if you have them handy.

**AWL** This tool is used for marking, punching holes for hardware, and manipulating small pieces when machine sewing.

**THREAD** Although you may want something bolder for decorative effects, *all-purpose polyester thread* will get you through most of the projects in this book, including those using lightweight leather. In addition to having a little more give than cotton, it's less likely to be degraded by the chemicals used for tanning leather. *Waxed linen thread* is not suitable for machine stitching, but makes particularly attractive hand stitches. If your store doesn't have it, *heavy-duty upholstery thread* is a decent alternative. Most domestic machines do not handle the combination of leather and heavy topstitching thread well, so if yours is struggling, you can also use a double thickness of all-purpose thread when you want a bolder line.

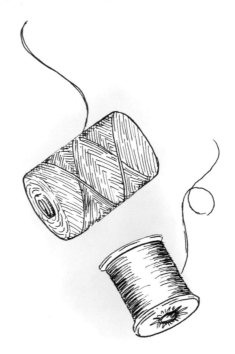

**HAND-SEWING NEEDLES** Buy a few variety packs of hand-sewing needles to try out, then stock up on your favorites so you can refresh when the one you're using gets bent, corroded, or dull. My standard choice for these projects is a size 9 embroidery needle, which is thin enough to pass through most materials easily but has a long eye that can accommodate a variety of threads. For heavy materials, I favor darners, which are similar but longer. Glover's needles are great for tough leather and nonwovens, but watch your fingers because they bite.

**MACHINE-SEWING NEEDLES** Choose universal needles for anything that doesn't seem inclined to give you guff. Use stretch needles for spandex and microtex needles for fine leathers (or denim needles if you want to use heavier decorative threads on leather). Only use leather needles for very tough materials because they make a larger hole that can weaken the material. Whichever needle you use, make sure that it's new and sharp. Machine needles get dull with use and can bend or acquire burrs if you sew over a pin or hit the needle plate. All of these things can reduce stitch quality, damage the fabric, or create mysterious snarls and thread nests. To head off these kinds of issues, pay attention to the sounds the machine and needle make as you stitch—a damaged or dull needle will start to make clunking noises as it punches through the fabric, so you can tell when it's time for a new one.

**GLUES** Grab a glue stick as a temporary adhesive for placing appliqués or holding leather seams while you sew, and get a water-based leather glue for permanently adhering hems and seam allowances.

**BONE FOLDER** This tool is helpful for making crisp creases in leather. Get a small size and it can also be used for turning out glove fingers.

**MALLET** I use mine for flattening leather seams, punching holes with a drive punch, and attaching hardware.

**SCREW PUNCH** This is my preferred tool for punching holes in leather straps and armor.

**CUTTING BOARD** Use this board with knives and punches to avoid marring your tabletop or damaging your tools.

**MACHINE FEET** In addition to the standard foot, you may want a *clear foot* for better visibility, a *roller foot* or *nonstick foot* for handling leather or coated fabrics, a *zipper foot* or *cording foot* for detailing, and a *straight-stitch foot* for very fine details. The *wheel-style roller foot* isn't available for all machines, but it's much more maneuverable than the standard roller foot.

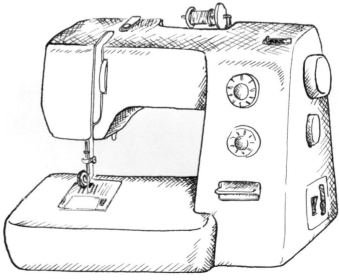

# BASIC SEWING TECHNIQUES

## HAND STITCHES

Hand sewing is a great way to keep control of small, fiddly pieces and narrow seam allowances. It's especially helpful when working with leather, which can be tricky to maneuver smoothly on a machine (and even more so in small sizes.) Although making an entire piece by hand can be time consuming, most glove and armwear projects are small enough to make it manageable. Many hand stitches can be used decoratively on external seams to emphasize a historical or finely handcrafted look.

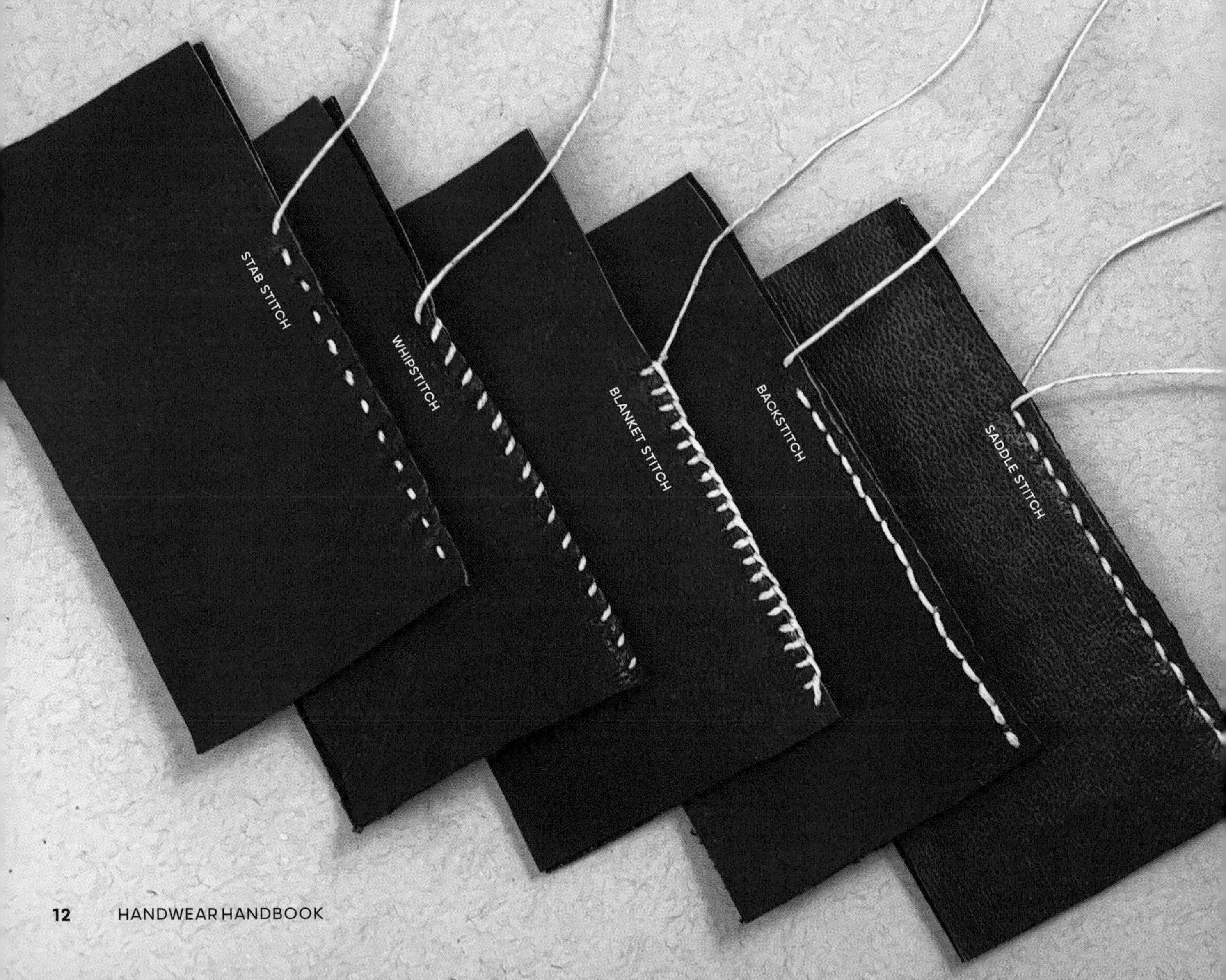

STAB STITCH

WHIPSTITCH

BLANKET STITCH

BACKSTITCH

SADDLE STITCH

A **STAB STITCH** looks like a basic running stitch, but you make each stitch meticulously one by one instead of stringing several together on the needle. This technique allows the stitches to enter perpendicular to the fabric, yielding smaller, more even stitches on thick materials like leather.

A **WHIPSTITCH** works well with narrow seam allowances and keeps them neatly contained. Each stitch enters the material in the same direction, and the thread wraps over the edge in between stitches. For sewing glove leathers, I find this stitch particularly effective when pulled tight, which draws the edge into a decorative scallop and helps keep the seams from "grinning" open on the reverse side. Use a doubled, heavy-duty, or button thread to reduce breakage when working this stitch.

A **BLANKET STITCH** is similar to a whipstitch, but each stitch also passes through the loop of the previous stitch. This technique causes the stitches to sit perpendicular to the edge and creates a decorative "bridge" of thread that sits just outside the seam allowance. It's useful for decorative effects, but it should be worked more loosely than the whipstitch to avoid seam puckering.

A **BACKSTITCH** is less ideal for seams that will be exposed on both sides because it's only attractive on one side, but it produces a very strong seam that can look machine stitched if done with enough precision. After the first stitch, the next stitch comes up a short distance away and enters again at the end of the first, creating a loop-the-loop structure that helps guard against snags and even allows the seam to stretch somewhat.

A **SADDLE STITCH** is like a stab stitch worked with two needles simultaneously on opposite sides so you get a continuous line of stitching instead of alternating stitches and gaps. Make sure that the needles both pass through the same hole each time and that your threads cross over each other in a consistent direction for the most even-looking stitches. It's a slow but very strong stitch that's common in leatherwork.

A **SLIP STITCH** is not ideal for construction seams that will be under tension, but it is often used for securing bindings, linings, and hems. Typically, the needle catches a fold of fabric on one side and just a few threads or a shallow scoop of material on the other, so the completed stitch is almost invisible on both sides.

A **CATCH STITCH** (also known as a *herringbone stitch* or *cross-stitch*) is another useful stitch for securing hems and loose edges. It's worked on alternating sides of the edge, with the needle inserted against the direction of stitching so that the threads cross with each stitch. This gives the stitch more flexibility than many alternatives, so it resists breaking when pulled. The formed "bridge" of thread helps to secure a loose edge or can even be used to make a channel for elastic or trim.

SLIP STITCH

CATCH STITCH

# MACHINE SEWING

Sewing on a machine is generally faster and easier than sewing by hand, but that doesn't always hold true for small, detailed projects or when you're manipulating tricky materials. You can absolutely sew gloves on a machine, and you can absolutely sew leather and stretch fabrics, too. But you might need a deeper bag of tricks to get good results with a minimum of frustration, so here are a few tips to get you started.

## Workspace

First of all, make sure you have very good lighting in your sewing area. Consider swapping in a superbright LED bulb if your machine still uses a standard one. You may even want a freestanding magnifying glass or magnifier lamp. Visibility is important, and if you find yourself leaning so close to the machine that you thump yourself in the forehead (just me?), that's a sign you need to adjust your workspace.

Next, take a look at your machine setup. If the machine allows it, you may wish to reduce the speed. A clear foot can be helpful for more visibility as you stitch, and some machines have the option of a straight stitch–only foot and needle plate that help prevent small pieces from being chewed up by the mechanism. Some vintage, industrial, and high-end machines also offer a knee lift mechanism, which is invaluable if you can get it because it allows you to raise and lower the presser foot while keeping both hands on your work.

## Working with Small Seam Allowances

Standard sewing machines are often set up to work with at least a ¼˝ (6mm) seam allowance, which is typical of quilting, or even wider than that for garment sewing. If you're using ⅛˝ (3mm) or less, the guidelines on the needle plate are basically useless and you will have to find your own reference points to keep the seam even. This may mean lining the edge of the fabric up with a certain point on the feed dogs or the foot itself, using a clear foot with lines drawn on it in fine-point permanent marker, or drawing in the exact stitching line on your material and lining that up with the needle. It can take some practice to keep your eye on the reference point and avoid being distracted by the movement of the needle, so keep at it until you can keep a consistent narrow seam width even around tight corners and curves.

## Machine Stitches

For small pieces, you'll have better control with a short stitch length (2mm or less). The exceptions to this are leather and leather-like fabrics, which will hold up better if you use a slightly longer stitch. If you are working with stretch fabrics, you'll want a stitch with some give to it. Specialized glove-making machines may accomplish this with a chain stitch, but most modern domestic machines have either a **TRIPLE STRAIGHT STITCH** (sometimes called a *backstitch, stretch stitch,* or *triple stretch stitch*) or a **LIGHTNING BOLT STITCH**, both of which use a back-and-forth stitch pattern to build stretch into the seam. These seams are typically slower to sew than the standard straight stitch, use more thread, and are more difficult to unpick if something goes wrong, but they make a nice-looking seam that won't pop if you yank on it. Zigzag stitches should be a last resort or reserved for finishing seams and applying elastic, as using them for construction will produce seams that "grin."

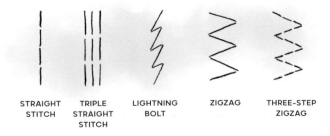

STRAIGHT STITCH · TRIPLE STRAIGHT STITCH · LIGHTNING BOLT · ZIGZAG · THREE-STEP ZIGZAG

### Feeding Tools

I sometimes use a large T-pin or sharp awl like a little claw to grip and manipulate small pieces, allowing me to control the material all the way up to the needle without risking my fingers. This maneuver can help fill the gap if the foot you're using doesn't grip the material firmly enough, which can cause skipped stitches. It also keeps layers moving together to prevent them from creeping as you sew, which can be a huge help when working with slippery, bias-cut, and napped fabrics.

## CONSTRUCTION TECHNIQUES

### Basic Seam

In most kinds of sewing, a basic seam is sewn with the right sides of the fabric together, and then the fabric is turned right sides out so that the seam allowances are hidden inside the garment. Seam allowances can range from ¼″ (6mm) to 1″ (2.5cm) or more and may require finishing with an overlock stitch, binding, or another method so that the fabric doesn't fray. For gloves, the seams may be sewn on the inside or the outside, depending on the material and the intended look, and typical seam allowances are ⅛″ (3mm) or less. With an unstable fabric, that tiny allowance would rapidly disappear to nothing, so most glove materials are chosen for their fray resistance, and the seams may be left unfinished for a softer, less bulky result.

INSEAM

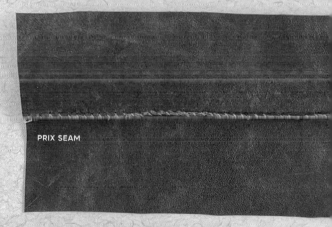

PRIX SEAM

### Lapped Seam

A lapped seam is an alternative to a standard seam, suitable for leather and other materials that don't fray and look reasonably attractive with a visible raw edge. In this method, one side of the seam is laid on top of the other, with a slight overlap of up to ¼″ (6mm), then sewn down the middle of the overlap. This is a great way to reduce stiffness and bulk in heavy fabrics or leather because the seam lies flat without requiring the material to fold back on itself. Lapped seams are also easy to sew in inset corners because you can simply line up the pieces in their finished position instead of having to pivot the corner. The trick is keeping the seam lined up correctly to sew because you can only see one of the edges while you work. To deal with this issue, I like to draw an overlapping line on the back of the upper piece, then line up the lower piece and glue it in place with leather or fabric glue before stitching.

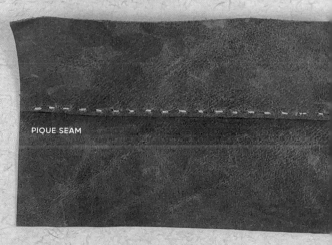

PIQUE SEAM

### Corner Pivots

Glove sewing will give you all the practice you could want at pivoting sharp corners on your machine. The main thing to remember is to always stop with the needle down so you can use it as an axis to pivot around without interrupting the line of stitching. Clip into the corner seam allowance before you begin so you can open the corner out straight as you sew. If you're working with a knit or woven fabric, you may need to stabilize the pivot point with a line of *stay stitching* a needle width from the final stitching line before you clip into it. This is usually a slightly longer stitch, sewn in the allowance where it will not be seen after the seam is sewn, for about 1″ (2.5cm) before and after the pivot point. This stitching prevents the fabric from stretching out or fraying at the corner, so you can cut very close to the stitching line without losing precision. (In most cases, you will not want to staystitch leather because the extra holes will weaken it.)

When you are sewing a convex corner into a concave one, it's usually easier to stitch with the concave side on top so you can hit the clipped corner more precisely. However, this is not always true. When inserting fourchettes in the back of a glove, it's easier to have the smaller piece on top so it doesn't get chewed up by the feed dogs.

Line up your first edge and stitch toward the corner, making sure that the pivot point lines up correctly on both layers. Hand crank the last few stitches if necessary to hit the dot exactly and stop at the lowest point of the needle's movement. Then lift the presser foot and pivot the fabric layers so the next line of stitching is lined up, making sure that any layers you don't want to catch are folded back out of the way. Continue stitching to the end of the seam.

## FINISHING SEAMS

When making gloves, it is more important to get a smooth, lump-free finish than to make the insides perfectly neat. Choose seam finishes like zigzagging, hand overcasting, or topstitching to control your seam allowances and minimize wear on the inside of your project without adding bulk or stiffness with a lot of extra fabric or thread. If you truly need a clean inside finish, or if the back side of your main fabric is too scratchy to wear as is, add a full lining in a thin, slippery fabric like tricot. Linings should be tacked to the outer glove at the fingertips in addition to being sewn into the hem so that they don't pull out when the glove is removed.

## HEMS AND EDGES

The simplest way to finish the edges of nonfraying fabrics is simply to turn the edges to the inside and topstitch them. With leather, the edges can also be glued down and rolled or hammered to make them extra flat. For lined gloves or with thicker knits, the hem can be invisibly hand stitched in place with a slip stitch or catch stitch. For a more substantial finish, you can bind or cord the edge. Bindings and cording can be purchased premade or made from matching fabric or leather.

## ELASTIC

On stretch fabrics, elastic is often used in place of a standard hem to stabilize edges so they don't stretch out. It's also useful for snugging in loose pieces on the wrist or arm and for creating shirred effects. Elastic in ¼″ (6mm) width is a good standard size for most handwear and armwear items, but you may want to go down to ⅛″ (3mm) for more delicate edges. Rounded cord elastic is more useful for decorative techniques (it can be used as a filler cord for piping) or as a drawstring for some kinds of athletic or performance gear. To attach elastic, you will want to use a zigzag or three-step zigzag stitch, which will allow enough stretch to avoid breaking but won't use so much thread that it interferes with the stretch.

## STRINGS AND STRAPS

Fabric or leather straps can be made by sewing a tube and turning it inside out, by folding raw edges in and securing them with a topstitch, or by sewing two layers together with raw edges exposed (with or without a layer of reinforcing material between them). You can also cut single-layer strips from a firmer material such as veg-tan (vegetable-tanned) leather and burnish or paint them to give a finished look. The specific material and situation will guide which method is most appropriate but, generally speaking, you want straps to be stable enough that they don't flop or curl. They should be slightly stiffer than the surrounding material, but not so heavy that they sag. If you are attaching buckles or other hardware, make sure the strap is stiff enough to support the weight of the hardware but thin enough to fit into the loops.

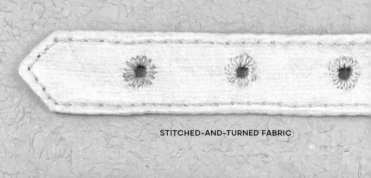

STITCHED-AND-TURNED FABRIC

DOUBLE-LAYERED LEATHER

LEATHER WITH FOLDED EDGES AND BACKING

SINGLE-LAYER LEATHER

# DECORATIVE TECHNIQUES

### Seam Details

In addition to the seams that give your piece shape, you may wish to add additional seams for decorative effect or color blocking. You can do this by cutting the pattern apart wherever you like and adding seam allowance to both cut edges, but think through the practicalities first. Will the shape be difficult to sew? Will the additional bulk or stiffness of the seam allowance interfere with other parts of the construction or with the function of the finished piece? If adding a standard seam isn't appropriate, you could consider using a flatter lapped seam or adding the detail with appliqué instead.

### Topstitching

One of the simplest ways to emphasize a seam detail, topstitching can also serve a structural role. Generally speaking, topstitching is a visible line of stitching near a seam or edge that often secures the surface layer of fabric to a seam allowance, lining, or other interior layer. It's not necessarily any more difficult to sew than a standard seam, but because it's intended to be visible it merits a little extra care to ensure the tension is correct, the stitching line straight, and the stitch length even. If you're joining multiple layers, make sure they don't skew as you stitch to avoid puckers or ripples between the rows of stitching. Topstitching that's ⅛″ (3mm) or less from a fold or outline is sometimes called edge stitching.

### Piping

Adding piping to a seam or edge gives it a bold, graphic outline but can also make it stiffer and bulkier. You can buy various types of piping premade, but you'll have more options if you make your own. Cut a strip of your decorative fabric along the bias (for wovens) or along the direction of the greatest stretch (for nonwovens, leather, and knits). The strip should be as wide as twice the seam allowance plus the width of fabric necessary to wrap around your filler cord, which can be any width you like but should be firm and smooth enough to create a defined shape. Cotton drapery cord, cord elastic, and satin rattail cord are good options depending on the desired stiffness and whether you need the piping to stretch. Fold the fabric around the cord and machine baste close to the edge with a zipper foot or cording foot (for fabrics) or hand baste or lightly glue (for leather). To apply, baste the cording in place along your stitching line on the front side of the fabric before sewing the seam. You may need to clip or pleat the seam allowance flange to shape the cording around sharp corners.

Alternatively, mark your placement line with chalk or a line of basting stitches and lay the piping down as you sew with a zipper or cording foot. This takes some practice but can save a lot of time and produce a more even result. Place your piped piece right sides together with the next piece of fabric and sew on top of the basting, or fold the seam allowance under and join the pieces by edgestitching next to the piping.

Before sewing the end of a piped seam into another seam or a hem, reduce bulk by clipping a few stitches just beyond the fold or seam line and pulling out the filler cord so you can trim away the portion that would cross into the seam allowance. To see this in action, check out the Leather Gloves project (page 68).

### Points

Three short pintucks called *points* are a traditional embellishment for the back of a pair of gloves that also help to shape the glove to the hand. They're easiest to do at the very beginning before the rest of the glove is put together.

Mark the beginning and end of the tuck and fold the material along the center line, then sew very close to the edge ($\frac{1}{16}$″–⅛″ or 1.5–3mm depending on the thickness of your material) between the endpoints. You can also sew pintucks with a twin needle, which uses two threads on the top side to produce identical parallel rows of stitching. The bobbin thread zigzags between them with every stitch and is pulled taut after stitching to draw the sides of the tuck together. If you are sewing by hand, especially in thicker materials like leather, a simple stab stitch produces an interesting wavy look.

If you are machine sewing, do not backstitch but leave thread tails long enough to pull to the inside and knot off. Use a hand needle to bury the knots and thread ends in the tuck. Note that the tucks do take up a bit of width from the hand, so start them below the widest part of the knuckles to leave that bit of extra space where it's needed.

### Quilting

Quilted details can be used to add dimension and texture to any area that doesn't need to be flexible. The main fabric is backed with a filler, which can be batting, fleece, flannel, or another lofty fabric that compresses well when stitched. The layers can be fused or glued to prevent shifting as you stitch. Finally, the pattern is created with rows or a grid of stitching that's worked from the center of the piece outward to reduce the chance of bubbles or puckers.

### Foam Padding

Padded areas can be created with a batting or filler fabric or with pieces of foam sandwiched between the outer fabric and a lining layer. If you are using EVA or craft foam, the shape of the piece will be sharply defined and you may wish to glue the layers in place to prevent shifting. Softer foams, like upholstery foam, will compress at the edges to make a more rounded shape. If you want to make your padded area as an appliqué, the easiest method is to assemble your fabric, foam, and a hidden backing, stitch out your shape, then cut the piece out close to the outline stitching and sew this self-contained unit onto your base fabric. This process avoids the difficulty of keeping springy layers aligned while trying to stitch a narrow edge.

### Cording

Somewhere between piping and quilting is cording, which uses rows of filler cord separated by lines of stitching to create a furrowed effect. A multichannel cording foot can help to make the lines more even. You can use the same kinds of cords that you would for piping, but some types can add a lot of stiffness to a piece, so make sure to experiment with samples and use this technique where the added structure will be beneficial.

### Appliqué

Both appliqué (a decorative piece sewn onto the base fabric) and reverse appliqué (decorative material sewn underneath and the top layer cut away) can be useful techniques for adding detail. They're especially simple when working with leather, which gives you clean-cut edges that do not fray or curl. For less stable fabrics, you can secure the edges by stitching over them with a dense zigzag or satin stitch, or by hand with a blanket stitch. Or you can turn the edges under and secure them invisibly with a slip stitch.

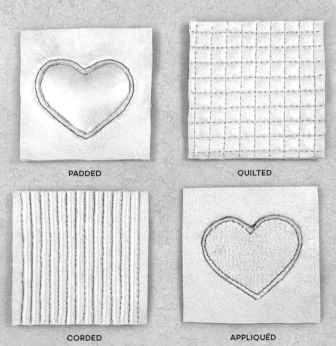

PADDED

QUILTED

CORDED

APPLIQUÉD

# FABRICS FOR HANDWEAR

## STABLE KNITS

Stable knits are easy to work with and do not fray, and they have enough give to allow for free movement, but not usually so much that it creates fitting challenges. Look for a dense knit made from thin yarns that doesn't show signs of runs, distortion, or raveling at the cut edge. It's also important to choose a fabric with good recovery that springs back to its original shape after stretching or the pieces you make from it will get loose and saggy as you wear them. Fabrics with the most stretch along either the lengthwise or crosswise direction are sometimes called two-way stretch, while fabrics with significant stretch and recovery in both directions are called four-way stretch. (Don't ask it to make sense.)

Knits often look better when sewn on a machine, as the very malleable material will show any lumps in the stitching line. For stable knits, you may want a ballpoint or jersey needle to avoid breaking threads as you stitch, as this can result in little holes in the fabric along the seam. If the knit has high spandex content, you may want a stretch needle instead. A short straight stitch will do the job just fine if the fabric is on the stable end with limited stretch, but you'll want to use a stretch stitch if the fabric stretches more than 10% or so in any given direction.

### CHECKING THE STRETCH RATIO

*To determine the stretch ratio of a fabric, fold it either parallel or perpendicular to the selvage. Place two pins perpendicular to the fold and exactly 10″ (25cm) apart. Lay a tape measure or yardstick on the table and pinch the fold with one pin in each hand. Stretch the fabric as far as it will go and check the new measurement. If your hands are now twice as far apart, your fabric has 100% stretch. If 10″ stretches to 15″ that's 50% stretch. Release the fabric and measure again to check its recovery—if it does not return to the original measurement, pieces made from the material may sag during wear. Repeat the measurement for the other direction before deciding how to cut your pattern. You always want greater stretch going around your hand to help with fit and mobility. Lengthwise stretch does not help significantly with the fit, but it can make the gloves more difficult to sew.*

## Common Stable Knit Types

**INTERLOCK KNIT** is commonly made from cotton, wool, and various synthetic fibers. It has a smooth, finely ribbed texture that resembles a T-shirt (jersey) knit, but is the same on both sides. It may have a little bit of mechanical stretch, so sometimes this fabric will give you a looser fit unless it has spandex in it to assist with recovery after stretching.

**PONTE KNIT** or **PONTE DE ROMA** is a medium- to heavyweight knit made with a mix of synthetic fibers. It may be smooth on both sides or have a fine crosswise rib pattern. Some ponte knits are prone to pilling over time, especially if they have a lot of polyester in the blend.

**SCUBA** is a thick, spongy synthetic knit made to mimic the look of neoprene. It's less expensive and easier to sew than the actual rubber and can be useful for a padded look or for creating textures with topstitching.

**NOVELTY KNITS** have more unusual textures or patterns and are suitable for glove making and similar projects as long as they're stable overall and resist disintegrating when cut. Large patterns may require careful placement when you are cutting small pieces so that you don't lose all the detail, but they're a great way to add interest and texture without a lot of extra work.

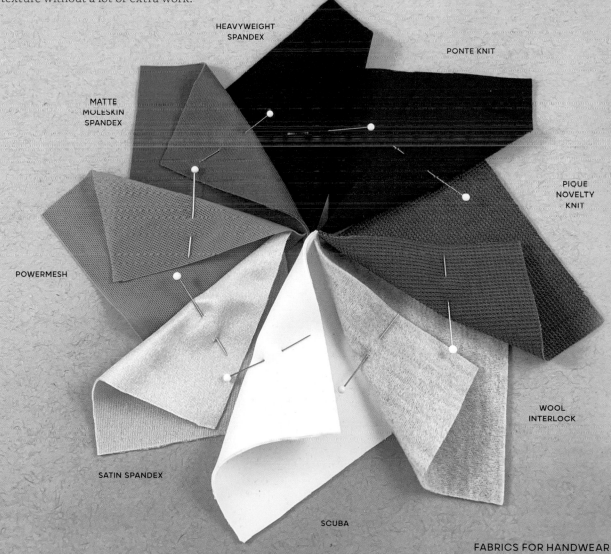

HEAVYWEIGHT SPANDEX

PONTE KNIT

MATTE MOLESKIN SPANDEX

PIQUE NOVELTY KNIT

POWERMESH

WOOL INTERLOCK

SATIN SPANDEX

SCUBA

# FOUR-WAY STRETCH KNITS

If you want a fabric with significant stretch and recovery in both directions, consider four-way stretch knits, which are made with a large proportion of spandex. Because they can stretch as much as 100% beyond their resting dimensions, they make it possible to simplify some kinds of patterns without completely ruining the fit.

While fitting is simplified with super-stretchy fabrics, the actual sewing can be a little harder. Always use a stretch stitch for seaming these fabrics or you'll risk popping stitches every time you pull the glove on or off. (A straight stitch does make an excellent basting stitch in stretch fabrics for this reason—it'll hold as long as you need it, but when you're done you can give the seam a yank to crack the threads and simply brush them away.)

If you find yourself struggling with skipped stitches, make sure you're using a stretch needle, which is designed with a deeper *scarf* (the indentation that looks like a bite out of the back of the needle) that makes it easier for the machine to form stitches. You can also try stitching on top of a piece of tissue or stabilizer, which prevents the fabric from "flagging" as you stitch and interfering with stitch formation.

You may also need a stabilizer to prevent the fabric from distorting and stretching as you sew, as this can cause misalignment of the pieces or make the finished seam look uneven and bumpy. Stabilizing materials are a common tool for machine embroidery, and many types are designed for easy removal from the fabric after sewing. Tear-away stabilizers work well for basic seams, and water-soluble types can be useful for situations with more complicated stitching or if you would otherwise end up with the stabilizer trapped between layers of fabric.

If you don't want to run out and buy something, you can also stabilize fabrics with freezer paper (which you can temporarily bond to the fabric by pressing with a low dry iron) or masking tape. Just make sure to remove any adhesives promptly after use as they can get gummy over time. Avoid using adhesive materials on leather or coated fabrics like faux leather or metallic spandex as you could damage the surface finish.

When buying stretch fabrics, always check both the stretch and the recovery as described in Checking the Stretch Ratio (page 20). Some stretch fabrics may become less opaque or appear a different color when stretched, especially those with prints that may reveal the underlying fabric color when stretched. This may be undesirable for projects that require a high degree of stretch or where the tension of the fabric may be uneven when worn, like the projects in Simplified Glove Patterns (page 53).

## Common Four-Way Stretch Knits

**MILLISKIN** is a lightweight knit made with a blend of nylon and spandex fibers. It has excellent stretch properties and is available in matte and shiny versions, but light colors may not be fully opaque.

**WET-LOOK SPANDEX** is made with shiny surface fibers that give a glossy effect. This can be a great option when you need a leathery look but want more stretch without the drawbacks of a coated fabric.

**METALLIC AND VINYL-COATED SPANDEX** have a nylon/spandex or polyester/spandex base fabric with a solid surface coating to give an ultra-glossy, leathery, or metallic look. These finishes are somewhat delicate and may rub off, crack, or peel with time, and any pin and needle holes are permanent so it's important to stitch accurately. The coatings can also increase the chance of having skipped stitches or fabric sticking to the machine. For special tricks to feed these knits, see Feed Issues (page 28).

**FOIL DOT SPANDEX** gives the look of a metallic or glossy surface but the surface coating is actually many small dots. This characteristic means it's less likely to show needle holes, and the coating is less likely to interfere with the stretch of the fabric. However, the foil finish is still delicate and it should be washed carefully and protected from abrasion.

**JUMBO SPANDEX** is similar to standard spandex but much heavier in weight. For small projects like gloves, it may be preferable to treat it like a stable knit because the very firm stretch may make it feel too tight otherwise.

**MICROFIBER SPANDEX** has a soft, matte surface and may have special performance or moisture-wicking properties. You may notice that the very thin fibers tend to snag on any rough spots on your hands.

**STRETCH MESH** is transparent, so seams should be neatly finished and as narrow as possible. It comes in a wide variety of colors and can be used as a substitute for body paint when cosplaying nonhuman skin tones.

Many of these stretch knits have a subtle nap to them, which means that their surface fibers have a preferred direction. The fabric feels smooth when you pet it one way and slightly rough or sticky the other way. A nap may cause subtle color differences depending on the orientation of the fabric and can make it difficult to keep pieces aligned if the direction of the fibers is competing, so it's best to lay your pattern out with all the pieces of fabric aligned the same way.

MILLISKIN

MICROFIBER

JUMBO SPANDEX

WET LOOK SPANDEX

FOIL MICRO DOT

METALLIC COATED SPANDEX

METALLIC STRETCH MESH

## WORKING WITH WOVENS

The vast majority of your average fabric store is filled with woven fabrics. They are available in a multitude of fibers and blends and range from whisper-frail gauze to droopy, liquid charmeuse to cardboard-stiff canvas. But nearly all wovens consist of distinct and separable warp and weft fibers, and as a result, they tend to fray at least a little when cut. Wider seam allowances are required to prevent the seams from pulling apart, so while these materials may work for some of the projects in this book, they tend to be less suitable for glove making.

This is not to say that making gloves from wovens is impossible, and sometimes you really need to match a specific fabric. In these cases, there are three steps you can take to maximize your chances of success: Choose a tightly woven fabric that frays as little as possible, finish your seams with a tight whipstitch or zigzag and add a dab of fray stopper to secure any remaining loose threads, and cut your pieces on the bias (at a 45° angle to the selvage or finished edge of the fabric) to both reduce fraying and allow some stretch from an otherwise rigid material.

## INTERFACING AND STRUCTURE

Most structured fabric pieces, like cuffs, gauntlets, and bracers, will benefit from some kind of additional support. Interfacings range from very fine knits (useful for stabilizing a limp fabric or adding a little extra strength to a fragile one) to heavy craft weights and thermoplastics that can hold a shape all on their own. A good repertoire will allow you to choose the most effective support material for your intended effect, supporting and enhancing the best properties of your outer fabrics.

Many interfacings come in both fusible and nonfusible versions (sometimes called sew-in interfacing). Fusible interfacings have a heat-activated glue on one or both sides so that you can permanently bond them to your fabric with an iron. Nonfusible interfacings can be applied by basting, quilting, or gluing them to your materials and include materials made specifically for the purpose as well as standard fabrics with structural properties, like silk organza or cotton canvas. You can also purchase fusible adhesive separately as a freestanding web, with or without a paper backing, for use with any fabric that can tolerate the heat. For items that will be washed frequently, nonfusibles may be more likely to maintain their properties over time, and fusibles should be secured with stitching where possible. Fabrics with a lot of stretch are more likely to peel away from a fusible backing unless the fusible has a similar amount of stretch.

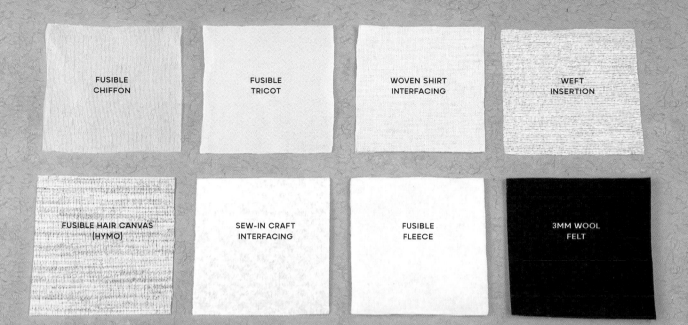

FUSIBLE CHIFFON

FUSIBLE TRICOT

WOVEN SHIRT INTERFACING

WEFT INSERTION

FUSIBLE HAIR CANVAS (HYMO)

SEW-IN CRAFT INTERFACING

FUSIBLE FLEECE

3MM WOOL FELT

## Interfacings to Know

**ULTRA-LIGHTWEIGHT INTERFACINGS** you're likely to encounter include silk-weight tricot and fusible chiffon. These interfacings are ideal when you want to stabilize a material without removing its drape, although the glue alone will give limp fabrics a little more body. They can also be used on the back of a slightly too-translucent fabric to make it more opaque.

**TRICOT INTERFACING** is a lightweight knit interfacing with considerable stretch in one direction. It's a good choice for most light- to medium-weight fabrics and can add strength and stability to whole pieces or reinforce high-stress areas.

**SHIRT INTERFACINGS** are still fairly thin, but they have a papery crispness that's used to support cuffs and collars. Use them to give a shirt-style cuff its characteristic sharpness, to reinforce straps, and to add smallish gauntlet details on gloves.

**TAILORING INTERFACINGS**, like weft insertion interfacing and fusible canvas, are heavier and sturdier and good for supporting large or heavily embellished gauntlets on historical-style gloves. When you work with bulky interfacings, it's a good idea to trim the interfacing out of the seam allowance so you don't end up with multiple layers in some areas.

**NONWOVEN CRAFT INTERFACING** is stiffer and bulkier still; it's good for fabric-wrapped bracers and pieces that bridge the gap between clothing and armor. It doesn't quite stand up by itself, but it does hold a defined shape. To avoid lumps, any seams in the interfacing should be laid together edge to edge, with no seam allowance or overlap, and joined with a zigzag stitch that straddles the seam.

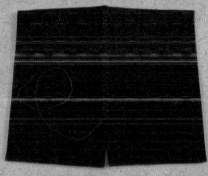

**FUSIBLE FLEECE** is bulky but flexible; it's good for lightly padded pieces and quilted details. It can also be used as smoothing padding to prevent understructure materials, like wire or boning, from showing through the outer layer.

**INDUSTRIAL FELT** is heavy wool or synthetic felt, typically available in 3mm or 5mm thicknesses. It can be sewn edge to edge with a zigzag stitch and is good for building substantial freestanding structures like paws or soft armor.

# LEATHER

Although many other options now exist, leather remains an ideal glove-making material: It is tough, flexible, and breathable, and it grips well and does not fray. Public demand for gloves once fed a proliferation of specialty leathers and the development of new tanning techniques, and some "wet glovers" did their own tanning in addition to cutting and stitching the finished material.

## SHOPPING FOR LEATHER

Most of us don't have access to the specialty leathers used by high-end glove makers, but you can still find some good options if you know what to look for. When you start shopping for leather, you'll most likely see two main types: garment leather and tooling leather. *Garment leather* may be cow-, sheep-, goat-, or pigskin treated with a chrome-tanning process that leaves the material soft and flexible. For most glove making, you're looking for very thin garment leathers, less than 2 ounces or ⅟₃₂″ (0.8mm) thick, so make sure you select something strong, stretchy, and resistant to tearing. Thicker leather may require careful construction choices to minimize bulk and preserve mobility, and it gives a heavy-duty protective look. The other common type of leather, *tooling leather* or *vegetable-tanned leather*, is more suitable for bags, belts, and other accessories than for clothing. It comes in various weights but tends to be on the thicker side, and it is stiffer and not very elastic. Use it for armor pieces on which you want to add detail through carving, stamping, and sculpting.

It's best to shop for leather in person, if possible, especially if you're not familiar with different types and weights and what they feel like, as a poor leather choice can easily make for an unwearably stiff glove. Old leather clothes from the thrift store or flea market can be a great resource if you don't have a leathercraft supplier near you, especially since glove pieces are small enough that you can easily work around damaged or stained areas (or not, if you want a head start on weathering a costume.)

## PREPARATION AND CUTTING

You can't necessarily discern the direction of a piece of leather by looking at it the way you might with fabric. But it does have a grain, running roughly from nose to tail, which can cause it to stretch more in the cross direction and affect the fit of pieces cut from it. It also has natural variations in thickness and stretch across its surface, which can change the characteristics of pieces cut from different areas. At a minimum, you want to make sure you cut a pair of tranks with the same orientation and from similar parts of the leather so that you end up with a matched pair. Fine glove makers go further and prestretch the leather along the direction that the gloves will be cut so that the lengthwise dimension starts out stretched to its maximum and all the give goes around the hand. This helps to prevent the strain of pulling the gloves on and off from lengthening them over time.

For purely decorative pieces, or where the stretch of the leather is less crucial to the fit of the finished object, you can lay out your pattern in whatever way will make the most efficient use of the material. It's best to trace your pattern pieces on the back side so you don't have to worry about getting rid of marks later, but do inspect the front side before you begin. Since leather is a natural material, it's pretty normal for it to have scars, holes, creases, thin spots, and other flaws that you want to avoid when cutting. Mark the positions of any flaws on the back so you can tell where they are when you lay out your pattern. Watch out for color variations as well, since different parts of the hide may take dye differently.

If you need to lay out your work on the front side of the material—for example, if there is a printed pattern or surface texture that requires specific placement—make sure you only mark where the lines will be cut away, or else use a marking implement that can be wiped away later. (My preferred white or silver gel pens can be removed from most surfaces with a damp cloth, but always test on a scrap first since different surface finishes will respond differently to both ink and water.)

## PINNING AND STITCHING

To avoid scarring the leather, any pins should be placed directly along the line of stitching where any holes will be covered by thread (remember to remove them as you sew, or you risk breaking needles and jamming the machine). Many people like using mini sewing clips in place of pins, but I often find them too clumsy for the most meticulous assemblies (although I do use them to secure glued pieces while they dry and keep small pieces and patterns organized). You can also substitute binder clips or paper clips if you don't have specialty clips handy. To avoid leaving imprints on delicate leathers, slip a scrap of cardstock between the leather surface and the clip.

The use of adhesives is one of the most significant differences in my work style when I switch from fabric to leather. Most leathers don't tolerate heat well enough to use fusibles, which would be the default choice for fabrics. And while tapes are neater to apply, most will gum up the needle if you stitch through them. However, a standard glue stick from your office supplies can work beautifully when you just need a temporary hold, and water-based leather glue is great for a more permanent option. Contact adhesives, which stick instantly if applied to both sides and allowed to dry until tacky before joining, have a powerful hold and can be extremely useful for trickier assemblies. But the best contact cements are solvent-based and very toxic, and they should only be used in a ventilated space with appropriate breathing protection. Nearly all glues will stick less effectively on the smooth finished side of the leather, so you may need to prepare the surface with leather deglazer or scuff up the area to be bonded with sandpaper if you want a permanent hold.

You may be tempted to run out and buy glover's needles or leather needles for machine sewing, both of which have a bladed tip that will chew through leather and your fingertips with equal ease. Unless your leather is particularly thick or tough, you can do just fine with standard needles, which also make smaller holes that are less likely to tear under stress. For machine sewing, microtex needles are a good option. They're thin and sharp and designed to slip through dense fabric. If you need to accommodate a thicker thread, try denim needles. Skipped stitches may mean you need a different needle type or a larger needle that will let the thread move more freely through the material.

Leather is a fairly strong material but will be weakened by stitching that is too dense (imagine perforated pages in a notebook). You want your needle holes to be small enough and far enough apart that the stitches won't tear out under tension. As much as possible, you should avoid redoing stitches or stitching back over the same areas. At the ends of your seams, leave long thread tails to knot off by hand instead of backstitching, then use a hand needle to thread the ends back through your other stitches. With synthetic thread, like nylon, you can carefully melt the ends with a lighter or candle to keep knots from coming undone.

## FEED ISSUES

Leather is notorious for sticking to the sewing machine bed and foot, which can inhibit feeding and make your stitch length uneven. It can even stick to the needle, causing *flagging*, which is when the material flaps up and down as you stitch, sometimes significantly enough to interfere with the stitch formation and cause skipped stitches.

Putting tissue paper above and below your leather layers is a very effective way to allow leather to feed freely through your machine and requires no extra equipment. Low-tack painter's tape can also do the job for more targeted areas, although it should be removed promptly after stitching to avoid damaging the surface finish of the leather. Both options are most useful for straight seams without much detail because the additional materials can obscure your work or reference marks and make it more difficult to maneuver accurately. And although it's usually easy enough to tear away the paper after you're finished stitching, it can mess up your tension and make the stitches look uneven.

Depending on the selection of feet available for your machine, you may have access to a nonstick foot that glides over sticky materials or one of a few different styles of roller feet. The wheel type can be hard to find, but is highly maneuverable and makes it easy to see what you're doing. The more common domestic type works well in most situations, but the knurled roller can mar delicate surface finishes. A walking foot, which uses the movement of the needle bar to raise and lower with each stitch, can be useful in certain situations but often does not grip the fabric as firmly and can exacerbate flagging issues.

Controlling the material manually is also an important part of working with leather and, really, any tricky fabric. This is something that comes with practice and developing a "feel" for the specific materials you're using. You need to hold all the layers together firmly enough that they don't creep and stretch out of place. And be ready to intervene if the machine balks so that the material isn't damaged by stitching over and over in one place. Although, generally, it's a bad idea to yank on your fabric while stitching, many domestic machines will need a little extra help to feed heavy layers. While a little bit of manual pressure can help to nudge your machine through these trouble spots, this should be done with extreme care to avoid breaking needles or interfering with the machine's timing.

NONSTICK FOOT

ROLLER FOOT

WHEEL ROLLER FOOT

CLEAR FOOT

STRAIGHT STITCH FOOT

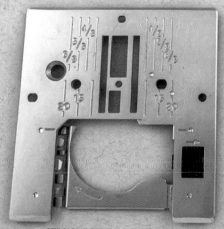

STRAIGHT STITCH NEEDLE PLATE

STANDARD ZIGZAG NEEDLE PLATE

## SEAM BULK

Even very lightweight leather tends to be on the thick side compared with most fabric, and it is less compressible. That means you need to be aggressive about dealing with bulk, especially when you have multiple layers or folded edges in the mix.

Seams in leather will often look better if they are flattened or hammered after sewing. This process is similar to pressing seams in conventional fabrics, but without heat or steam since leather scorches easily. You will need a heavy roller, bone folder, or smooth mallet and a hard, smooth surface to hammer on since any texture may imprint on the leather. After hammering, you can glue the seam allowances down with leather glue to keep them neat and flat.

Topstitching or edgestitching is another way to flatten edges and seam allowances in leather, and also works decoratively to make pieces look crisp and finished. If machine topstitching doesn't feel like it suits your character's genre, you can do a pick stitch or backstitch by hand—but note that a well-balanced machine stitch can look very similar to a hand saddle stitch, which is a perfectly traditional choice for leatherwork.

Many domestic machines struggle to feed in areas where there is an abrupt transition in thickness, like when you're starting a thick seam or stitching over a seam intersection. Your machine may skip stitches or maul your leather as it stitches over and over in place. You can use little chips of cardboard or offcuts from your project to level out the thickness so the foot stays level and everything feeds smoothly, especially if your machine struggles at the beginning of thick seams. Where possible, create a smooth slope at seam intersections by grading your seam allowances (trimming the layers of seam allowance at slightly different widths so that the edges don't all line up and create a cliff) or hammering the seam flat. Otherwise, use a pin or awl to hold the layers down firmly so that the feed dogs can keep a firm grip and nothing can lift or flap with the needle's motion.

For very chunky leathers, you may need to *skive* (shave away some of the thickness of) the edges to get a neat transition at the seam. This requires a very sharp specialized knife or razor blade and needs to be done carefully to avoid compromising the strength of the seam. Although rarely necessary for garment leathers, it can add some finesse to thicker armor pieces.

## LEATHER-LIKE MATERIALS

Faux leather and leather-like synthetic materials are generally less expensive than real leather and may be more readily available. Some people prefer to use them for philosophical reasons as well, although this is a complicated issue with many trade-offs.

Faux leather, or pleather, is a knit or woven fabric base coated in a skin of polyurethane or vinyl, often with an embossed texture that imitates the grain of natural leather. The knit version is preferable for gloves, but the woven version is still moderately fray resistant thanks to the coated surface. Both should be handled carefully as stitching or pinning holes will be permanent and any damage to the coating can cause it to peel away from the backing (either immediately or over time.)

On the less realistic end, gloss vinyl and metallic foil fabrics handle in much the same way as faux leather. Just make sure you're picking fabric-backed materials as opposed to those with fuzzy felt-like backing like upholstery vinyl.

Faux suede is a synthetic knit, woven, or nonwoven fabric with a brushed surface intended to look like actual suede. For glove making, the knit and nonwoven versions are preferable to prevent fraying. It's up to you whether you prefer the thinner, stretchier knit version or nonwoven materials like Ultrasuede, which may be more convincing fakes, but are also more rigid (and often expensive).

Nonwoven suede materials are less likely to show permanent holes than coated fabrics, but they may still be weakened if your stitching is too dense in any particular area.

When it comes to working with these materials, many of the techniques used for leather are also appropriate for the synthetic imitators. Solutions for minimizing holes and ensuring smooth feeding will also apply. However, synthetic materials are typically more difficult to glue. If you need a temporary adhesive, low-tack painter's tape can be a useful way to hold pieces in place for stitching, although it should be removed promptly afterward so it doesn't damage the surface or become gummy. For a permanent hold, water-based adhesives are unlikely to be adequate and you should skip straight to contact cement, following the appropriate surface preparation steps and safety precautions (see Pinning and Stitching, page 28).

TEXTURED METALLIC FAUX LEATHER WITH KNIT BACKING

NONWOVEN FAUX SUEDE

FAUX SUEDE SCUBA KNIT

WOVEN-BACKED FAUX LEATHER

SMOOTH FAUX LEATHER WITH KNIT BACKING

METALLIC COATED SPANDEX

# BASIC PROJECTS

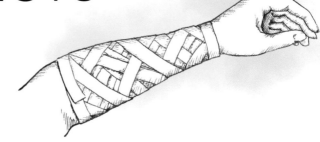

## MAKING AN ARM FORM

Fitting pieces on your own arms can be difficult, and many projects require a basic shape to build your project around to ensure that it will fit once it's done. While it's technically possible to buy arms for dress forms and mannequins, there's very little reason to do so when you can make your own with either a very simple approximation or a true copy of your own arm.

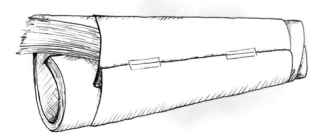

### Dead Simple Arm Form

Start by measuring your forearm around the wrist and elbow and along the length between them. Mark these dimensions on a large piece of heavy paper, cardstock, or oak tag paper, making a roughly trapezoidal shape, then fold the excess paper to the back along one lengthwise edge. Roll the paper into a tube, matching the folded edge to your other pair of marks, and tape it in place. Next, take a thick magazine and roll it up slightly smaller than your arm tube, with the spine toward the inside so the splayed pages create a smooth shape. Slide it in and allow it to unfurl so that it firmly fills the arm tube. (You can substitute a large piece of stiff paper if you don't have a magazine handy.)

### Tape Wrap Arm Form

The slightly more involved version requires gummed paper tape from the office supply store—the kind that activates with moisture like an envelope. You will also need plastic cling wrap, safety scissors, and a friend to wrap your arm. Set out a shallow tray of water with a sponge or folded paper towel in it for activating the tape, and precut a stack of tape pieces in various sizes. You will want some narrow strips to contour to the shape—about ½″ (1.3cm) by at least 6″ (15.2cm) long—and some wider strips of about 1″ (2.5cm) to cover the area efficiently. Wrap as much of your arm as you intend to copy in cling wrap, then hold it still in a relaxed position while your friend wraps the tape.

Have your friend start with long, wide strips, spiraling up and down your arm both clockwise and counterclockwise to create a sturdy structure of crossed strips. The thinner strips should be used to get smooth coverage over curves, and the entire area should be covered with at least a few layers. The tape will harden as it dries, so leave it in place until it feels firm enough to hold its shape when you cut it off your arm. Use a marker to draw in useful guidelines, like the elbow and wrist, then carefully cut the form off your arm using safety scissors. The form will be somewhat larger than your actual arm, so measure at your guidelines to determine how much to trim before you tape it back together. Stuff the form with paper to support it as it finishes drying, and when it's done, you'll have a hard, lightweight form that's easy to draw on and pin into.

## Tape Wrap Patterns

Wrapping yourself in tape is also one of the easiest ways to make a form-fitting pattern, and it is especially convenient for making small pieces like bracers, which can be made on your nondominant arm and don't require much tape. To make a pattern instead of a durable form, use flexible tape like masking tape or duct tape. You can also use a marker to draw in details (or at least some guidelines) before cutting the piece off of yourself with safety scissors. For more elaborately detailed pieces, you may wish to make a form first and do your pattern wrap on that instead of on yourself.

Once you have your tape shell in hand, identify any domed areas. Add seams across the peaks of the domes until each piece lies flat. Or you can leave your pattern in one or a few pieces and add shape with a dart cut from an edge to the peak, allowing the piece to open up in a wedge shape that will be sewn back together like a partial seam. For very curved areas, you may need multiple darts, as very wide wedges will not sew up nicely in all materials. To make a pattern for a stretch fabric, you can sometimes flatten the curved parts instead of cutting into them, but in rigid materials, this will result in finished pieces that are too small.

Copy the tape pattern onto paper for your actual working pattern, as tape distorts too easily and may give you an asymmetrical pair of patterns for left and right pieces. You can smooth out irregularities when cleaning up the lines, but be careful not to change the overall fit. If you are working with nice fabric that you can't get more of, make a mock-up first with a less precious material in case you need to adjust anything.

# Embellished Cuffs

This super-simple wrist cuff is just a collection of rectangles, embellished into a wearable confection. In soft colors, it makes a great accessory for a fluffy dress, or with a palette change, it can look dark and gothic. For bonus coordination points, you can make the whole thing with scraps and leftover embellishments from the rest of your outfit.

## MATERIALS

*½ yard (46cm) lightweight cotton such as voile*

*¼ yard (23cm) lightweight knit or woven interfacing*

*1 yard (91cm) scallop-edge lace trim*

*1 yard (91cm) ribbon*

*2 buttons ½″ (1.3cm)*

*Fabric flowers*

*Beads, rhinestones, or other sparkly embellishments*

## PATTERN AND CUTTING

First, measure your wrist loosely, using the tape as a stand-in for the final cuff to determine what size will be both secure and comfortable. Add 1″ (2.5cm) for an overlap. Draw a rectangle using this length and 1¼″ (3.2cm) for the width. Add a ⅝″ (1.6cm) seam allowance to all four sides. (The seam allowance will fill the cuff once it's turned out, so the band has a little more substance and a less dramatic lump at the edges.)

Cut 4 cuff pieces and apply interfacing to 2 of them. Cut 2 ruffles 3½″ × 30″ (8.9cm × 76.2cm) and 2 ruffles 1½″ × 30″ (3.8cm × 76.2cm). Cut the lace at about 18″ (46cm), but adjust the length so that it cuts off at a nice point on the scallop at both ends.

## CONSTRUCTION

**1.** Starting with the wide ruffle piece, sew a narrow double-fold hem on one long edge and both short ends. The narrower you can make this hem, the more elegant it will look. You can fold and press by hand, or use a rolled hem foot on your machine. Mark your stitching line along the other long, unhemmed side at your preferred finished width. Here, it's 2¾″ (7cm).

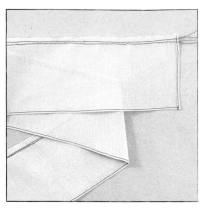

**2.** For the lace, which doesn't fray but looks a little nicer with a finished edge, pick a good stopping point in the scallop. Fold the end under, straight stitch right next to the fold, and trim very close to the stitching.

**3.** Zigzag across the hem to pull it into a small, neat roll. In the example, metallic gold thread was used to mimic the finished edge of the lace.

**4.** To sew two rows of gathering stitches along the top of the wide fabric ruffle, set your machine to its longest straight stitch and reduce the tension a notch or two. Stitch the first row one needle width from the marked seam line, and the second row about ¼″ (6mm) into the seam allowance. Leave long thread tails at both ends and do not backstitch.

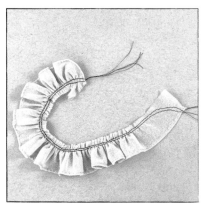

**5.** Gently pull the bobbin threads to gather, working the folds along the length of the seam until they're evenly distributed and the total length matches your lace measurement. Then pull the top threads through to the back side and knot them off. Pin the fabric ruffle to the lace and sew another two rows of gathering stitches through both layers.

**6.** To avoid hemming the short edges of the narrow top ruffle, you can curve the gathering threads down toward the hem. Once gathered, the ruffle rounds smoothly to nothing at the end.

**7.** Gather the combined ruffle and the top ruffle to your finished cuff measurement.

**8.** Pin the ruffles along the top and bottom edges of the interfaced cuff piece, remembering to leave the seam allowance clear at both ends, and stitch just below the gathering stitches. Press the seam allowances flat with the edge of the iron to avoid crushing the ruffles.

**9.** Arrange ribbons or flat lace trims on the interfaced side of your cuff, and stitch them down by hand or machine. The trims extend into the seam allowance on the short edges but should stay clear along the long sides.

**10.** Along one long edge of the cuff lining, fold the seam allowance up and press. Lay the lining on top of your cuff, folded edge toward the lower ruffle and right sides together, with the top ruffle sandwiched between the cuff layers. With the lining as the top layer, stitch through everything along the top and both short ends, pivoting at the corners and being careful to not catch the top ruffle in the short end seams.

**11.** Clip the corners, turn out, and press. Align the folded edge of the lining so that it just covers the stitching line of the lower ruffle and pin or baste. Then stitch in the ditch from the outside to secure.

**12.** Add ½" (1.3cm) buttonholes on one end of each cuff (remember to mirror them so you get a pair). Wrap the cuff around your wrist to mark the button position and sew the button in place.

**13.** Sew on fabric flowers and beads by hand, or apply any other adornments you prefer.

# Buckled Arm Warmer

Arm warmers jangling with hardware are an Alt fashion staple, but if you change up the fabrics and fastenings, you can create all kinds of looks. Swap the buckles for a more convenient zipper if you don't like fuss, or add grommets and laces for a rustic or corsetry-influenced look.

The example version is made in faux suede, which allows the straps to be cut and stitched flat with the edges left raw. You can make this piece with a woven fabric, but you will need to select a nonfraying contrast fabric or leather for the straps or sew them with a seam allowance and turn them out.

## MATERIALS

*½ yard (46cm) outer fabric*

*½ yard (46cm) lining*

*½ yard (46cm) medium-weight woven interfacing for the straps*

*10 buckles ¾˝ (2cm)*

*Screw punch or drive punch and mallet*

*Nonstick sewing machine foot*

*Printed buckle strap pattern*

### Buckle Strap Pattern

To access the Buckle Strap Pattern piece through the QR code at right, open the camera app on your phone, aim the camera at the QR code, and click the link that pops up on the screen.

To access the pattern through the tiny url, type the web address provided into your browser window. tinyurl.com/11509-pattern1-download

## CREATING THE PATTERN

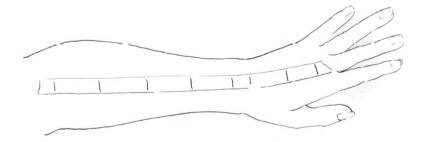

**1.** Lay a piece of masking tape along your forearm from your knuckles to your elbow. Make marks at your wrist bone, the top and bottom of of the intended thumb opening, and about every 2˝ (5cm) up the length of your arm. Then measure the circumference of your forearm at each point and record it on the tape next to the mark.

**2.** Transfer the tape to a piece of pattern paper. Using one edge of the tape as a center line, measure out perpendicular to each mark to one-quarter of the corresponding circumference measurement and connect the marks into a smooth curve. Draw in the top edge about 1″ (2.5cm) above the top of the thumb opening and the bottom edge at your preferred length.

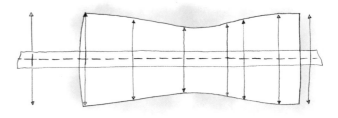

Add ¼″ (6mm) seam allowance to the sides, but nothing at the top and bottom edge as they'll be finished with a binding. Make a second copy of the same shape so that you have separate pieces for the outside (back of the hand side) and the inside (palm side) of the arm.

**3.** On the palm-side piece, draw in the thumb opening. This is roughly egg-shaped, with the narrowest point toward the finger end and about ¼″ (6mm) from the side seam. The widest part ends up about ⅛″ (3mm) from the side seam, with the opposite edge about halfway across the palm. You can adjust the shape and proportions of this opening to your liking, as long as there's enough room to fit your thumb through. (You can even cut the opening out of the paper pattern and try it on to see how it looks.) Add a ¼″ (6mm) seam allowance to the thumb opening.

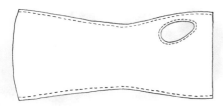

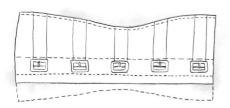

**4.** On the back of the hand piece, draw in a 1½″ (3.8cm) overlap along the center line for the buckle opening (this can be larger or smaller as you prefer). Cut along the overlap line on one side and add a ¾″ (2cm) hem allowance to both pieces. Lay the buckles on the pattern to determine where you would like the straps to be placed and draw in their positions.

**5.** For the straps, measure from the side seam to the center bar of each buckle. Add 2″ (5cm) to each measurement to allow a turnback to secure the buckle, plus some wiggle room for positioning. The strap pieces are cut as rectangles, using this measurement for the length and 2″ (5cm) for the width (twice the finished width plus the seam allowance). The strap interfacing will be cut to the same length, but a little less than the exact width of the finished strap.

**6.** The pointed tabs should be cut an additional 1½″ (3.8cm) longer than the corresponding buckle strap. Make a template for your desired end shape and the hole placement. Once centered on the exact measurement, add an additional hole ¾″ (2cm) on either side of the center for decoration and to allow for fit adjustment.

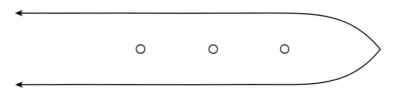

## CUTTING

Cut 2 palm pieces, and 4 each for the back of the hand pieces from the outer and lining fabrics, making sure to flip for a left and a right. On the lining pieces, trim away 1″ (2.5cm) from the overlap edge on the back of the hand pieces to ensure the lining stays rolled to the inside. Cut 4 bias strips 1½″ (3.8cm) from the outer fabric, each long enough to finish the top and bottom edges. Also cut 20 rectangles 2″ wide (5cm) for the straps, plus 20 strips of interfacing ¹¹⁄₁₆″ wide (1.8cm), using the length measurements determined above for both.

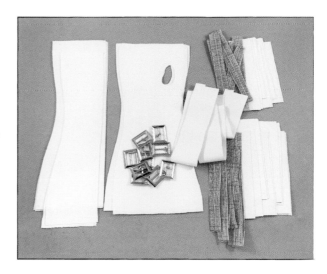

## CONSTRUCTION

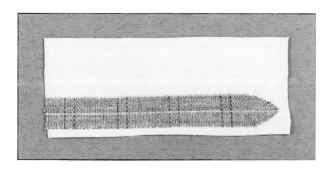

**1.** Use the strap end template to cut half of the strap interfacing pieces into the point shape. Adhere the interfacing near one edge of each strap piece, leaving a ¼″ (6mm) seam allowance at each pointed end. Fold the straps in half lengthwise along the middle of the fabric, enclosing the interfacing, and stitch right at the edge of the interfacing down the two long edges of the straps and around the points (for the buckle straps, just stitch down the long edges.) Trim very close to the stitching so that the finished strap ends up the correct width for the buckles.

**2.** Use the template to mark the holes on the pointed straps, then cut them with a screw punch or drive punch and mallet.

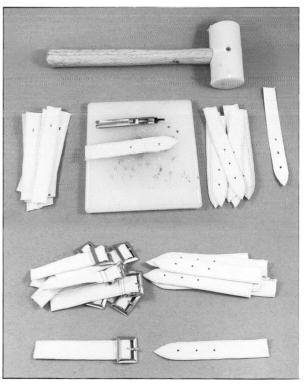

**3.** Punch two holes right next to each other about 1″ (2.5cm) from the end of the buckle strap and cut between them to make an oval-shaped opening. Feed the short end through the buckle, double it back, and topstitch with a zipper foot to secure.

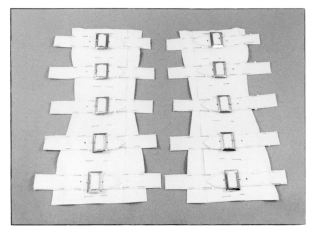

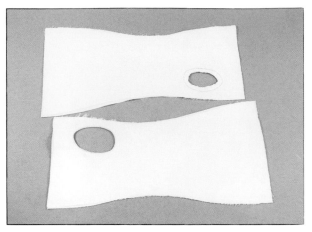

**4.** Overlap the pieces for the back of the hand by 2¾″ (7cm) for the finished overlap plus the hem allowance, and pin them together. Feed the tabs into the buckles and arrange them on top, following the marks you made earlier. Pin perpendicular to the edge on each side of each strap, baste within the seam allowance to secure, then trim away the excess strap length.

**5.** Line up the palm and palm lining pieces with right sides together. Stitch around the thumb opening, clip, and turn out. Press flat, then understitch from the inside, holding the outer layer out of the way.

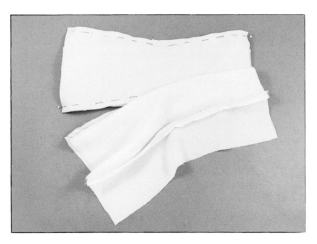

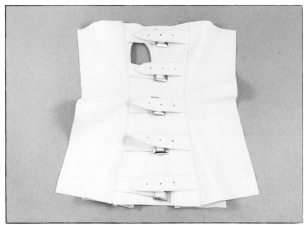

**6.** Unpin and unbuckle the upper pieces so they're separate again. Pin the palm lining to the lining for the back of the hand and the outer fabric to the outer fabric, right sides together with the strap ends caught between the outer layers, and stitch.

**7.** Press the seam open with the strap ends toward the palm. Edgestitch to force the straps to fold back on themselves when worn, which will create a little more separation between the straps and base so they're more visible.

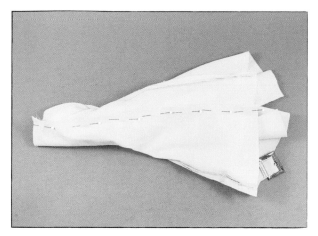

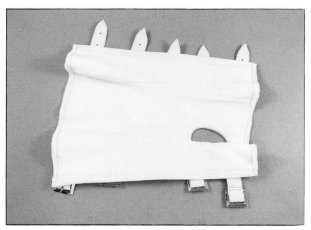

**8.** Lay the whole piece out flat with the outside up. Take both outer and lining layers on one side and fold them toward the middle, then wrap the other lining over the top and the outer underneath to meet it so that the entire piece is sandwiched between the outer and lining layers. Stitch with right sides together and a ¼″ (6mm) seam allowance and press.

**9.** Turn right side out and repeat for the other side, then wrap around a seam roll and press. Since the lining was trimmed slightly shorter than the outer fabric, it should roll nicely to the inside. Pin the layers in place and baste ¼″ (6mm) from the top and bottom edges.

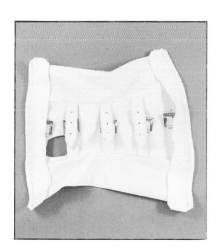

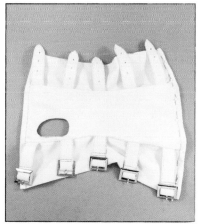

**10.** Stitch the binding strip to the outside at the top and bottom edges, right sides together, about ⅜″ (1cm) from the edge, leaving a little extra to fold in at each end.

**11.** Press the binding up, tuck the ends in, then fold it down twice to just cover the stitching. Stitch in the ditch from the outside to secure.

# Arm Wrap

Arm wraps are a popular look for costumes inspired by boxing and martial arts or as a historical method of securing loose sleeves so they don't get in the way. You could wrap yourself up with a long strip of fabric every time you wear the costume, but the simplest solution isn't necessarily the most practical. Instead, try building the wrap onto a fabric bracer that closes with a zipper. It'll be faster to get into, more comfortable, and less likely to fall down or slide out of place while you're wearing it.

## MATERIALS

½ yard (46cm) stable stretch knit with good recovery

Lightweight fusible knit interfacing

1 yard (91cm) textured woven cotton or linen for wrap

Curved hand needle

2 invisible zippers 10˝ (25cm)

2 small sew-on snaps

Fabric paint for weathering

Tape wrap arm form (page 32)

Heavy paper for spacer

Invisible zipper foot (recommended) or standard zipper foot

*This project needs an arm form to hold the shape while you stitch the wrap in place. If you haven't yet made the Tape Wrap Arm Form, this is a good time for a brief detour.*

## PATTERN AND CUTTING

Draw a line equal to the length of your inner forearm from wrist to elbow crease. Fold your pattern paper in half along this line. Measure around your wrist, the middle of your forearm, and just below your elbow, and multiply each measurement by 0.48 (this may be easier to do in metric measurements). Mark each measurement out perpendicular to the center line and connect the marks into a smooth curve. Draw in gentle curves as shown for the wrist and top edges, making sure the lines form a right angle at the center and each corner. Add a ⅜˝ (1cm)

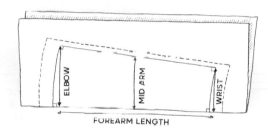

seam allowance to the side and about 1˝ (2.5cm) hem allowance to top and bottom (the ends toward your fingers and elbow).

Cut 2 of these base pieces from the stretch knit with the greatest stretch going around your arm. Cut your textured wrap fabric into 4˝ (10cm) bias strips (or whatever width you need to achieve your desired look). Cut 4 strips of fusible knit interfacing 1˝ (2.5cm) wide and as long as the distance from hem to hem.

## CONSTRUCTION

**1.** Apply the strips of fusible knit interfacing to the wrong side of the base pieces, centered on the stitching line.

**2.** Use a pin or chalk pencil to mark the hem allowance at the wrist and 2″ (5cm) down from the top edge. Position the invisible zipper facedown on the right side of the fabric, aligning the edge of the tape with the edge of the fabric and the top stopper with the hem line at the wrist.

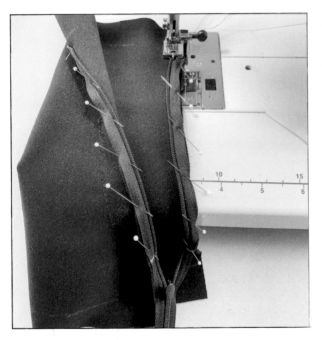

**3.** Open the zipper so the slider is out of the way, and fold the end of the tape under so that it doesn't extend into the hem allowance. Stitch both sides from the wrist toward the elbow, stopping at the mark, using an invisible zipper foot to get as close as possible to the teeth. (You can also use a standard zipper foot, but it's a little more work to keep the zipper in its unrolled position and get the stitching close enough to the teeth.)

**4.** Close the zipper and stitch the remaining 2″ (5cm) of the seam with a standard zipper foot. The end of the seam will be offset about a needle width from the zipper stitching, allowing the fabric room to roll so that you don't get a lump at the end of the zipper. Stitch the full length again at the edge of the zipper tape to secure it to the seam allowance so that it lies flat.

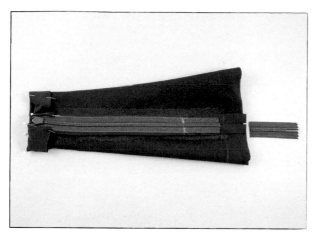

**5.** Trim the excess zipper tape at the top and bottom and fold the hem allowance down to cover the cut end.

**6.** Secure the hems at the top and bottom with a zigzag or triple-step zigzag stitch.

**7.** Turn the bracer base right side out and slide it onto your arm form with the zipper toward the inner arm where it will be the least visible. Fold the first bias strip in half lengthwise and begin wrapping at the top edge of the bracer base. Secure with hand pick stitches as you go, placing your stitches so that they will be covered by the next layer of the wrap. I find a curved needle to be especially effective for this kind of work, but you can use a standard needle if that's more comfortable. Since the stitching will hold the wrap in place either way, you can wrap in a tight, neat pattern or make it loose and haphazard depending on your intended look.

**8.** To make a spacer, cut a strip of heavy paper 2″ (5cm) wide and at least as long as your wrap. Fold in half lengthwise, then fold each raw edge back to meet the fold, creating a W shape.

Pin the spacer on top of the zipper so that the center fold sticks straight out and the outside edges lie flat against the arm.

**9.** Continue covering the base in rows, using the folded edge of the strip to cover the stitching and raw edges of the previous row. Leave the wrap loose enough at the inside of the arm to bridge the spacer without crushing it—you will need that space to finish it neatly at the end. Knot the thread on both sides each time you cross the spacer so that it won't unravel when you cut through it later.

**10.** When you come to the end of a fabric strip, cut it off where it would cross the spacer and start a new strip right next to it.

**11.** As you near the end, adjust your strip to fold roughly in thirds so that for the final row of the wrap you get a clean folded edge at both top and bottom that can be secured with a single line of pick stitches. Finish with a small tail at the wrist edge to cover the end of the zipper.

**12.** Baste along each side of the spacer line and then cut along the center fold.

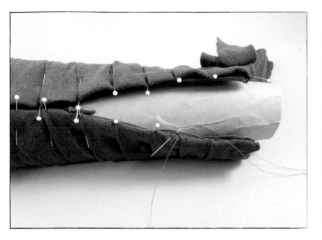

**13.** Fold the cut ends under along each side of the zipper, making sure that the strips align across the opening so that it will look as seamless as possible. Slipstitch everything in place. (You may find it easiest to pin one side, stitch, then match up and pin the other side.)

**14.** Fold the raw edges in and then into a triangle to close the end of the last trailing strip.

**15.** Slipstitch it closed and sew on the pronged side of a small snap. Lay this tab across the end of the zipper to cover the slider and pin. Slide the whole piece off the arm form and tuck the tab to the inside of the wrist, then mark and sew the snap socket so that it keeps the end tucked in.

**16.** If you wish, use fabric paints to weather the wrap and highlight the individual strips so they are more visible. Use a lighter color to pick out edges and folds and a darker, duller color for shadows to create depth. Here, I've used medium gray and dark navy fabric paints, applied lightly with a dry brush.

# GLOVES

The main difference between sewing gloves and sewing any other item of clothing is the level of precision needed. The average shirt pattern will still basically work if you're ⅛″ off in the seams, but with a glove pattern, that ⅛″ (3mm) can be the difference between a glove that fits and one you can't even get on. Gloves also use very small seam allowances, which is necessary because of the limited amount of space between the fingers, but again calls for precise cutting and stitching. There also isn't much room to adjust a glove once the pieces have been cut out, so if the finished glove doesn't fit, you may have to start over. Still, don't be intimidated—this is a matter of strategy and tools, not raw skill.

## FITS LIKE A ...

The first step in glove making is to measure carefully and adjust the pattern to fit. Since fingers can vary in both length and thickness, there are a lot of dimensions that can be customized, and few people will fit a pattern exactly as printed.

Start by drawing around each hand on a piece of paper. Draw reference dots on both sides of each fingertip, matching the fingertip notches of the glove pattern, and at the base of the web between each finger. On your drawing, record the distance between the dots on each side of each finger, as well as the circumference of each finger and your whole hand at the knuckles. Use a soft measuring tape if you have one handy, or measure with a strip of paper and then check it against a ruler. For imperial measurements, record to the nearest sixteenth of an inch; in metric, to the nearest millimeter.

Starting on the palm side of the pattern—the side with the thumb opening—cut across the finger portion of the pattern and adjust each finger individually so that the length is about ¼″ (6mm) longer than your measurement. Make sure you measure the actual stitching line, not the seam allowance, as they won't be the same. If the left and right sides of the fingers disagree, you can make fine adjustments by moving the fingertip dot up or down on each side.

Next, identify the corresponding half of each finger on the back of the hand (you can fold along the center line and match them up if that helps). Note that the two halves are not identical: The notch between the fingers is deeper on the back of the hand because of the shape of the finger webbing, while the tip is longer on the palm side to accommodate the curve of the fingertip. Don't force them to match, but simply make the same adjustment to each finger as you did on the palm. Do the same for each fourchette or gusset, remembering to make the same change on each side of the middle and ring fingers.

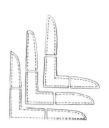

Check that the total width of the hand piece is large enough to go around the widest part of your knuckles and that the distance around each finger (including gussets) is sufficient. Remember that the forefinger and pinky will have one gusset each, and the other fingers will have two. If you need more or less of both hand width and finger width, you can carefully split each finger up the middle and add or subtract there. If you need more finger width only, make your adjustments by splitting the gussets as shown, then lengthening or shortening at the tip to restore the original length. If you just need to change the hand width, do that first and then alter the gussets in the opposite direction to keep the overall finger width the same. The wrist width can simply be adjusted at the side seams—it doesn't need to be super snug. Remember that if there is no vent or closure at the wrist, you will need to make it wide enough to fit your hand through or you won't be able to get the glove on.

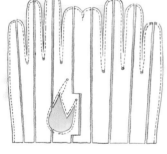
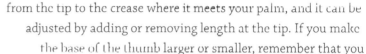

Check the length and circumference of your thumb against the thumb pattern. The length of the thumb piece should equal the length of your thumb along the outside from the tip to the crease where it meets your palm, and it can be adjusted by adding or removing length at the tip. If you make the base of the thumb larger or smaller, remember that you will need to alter the thumb hole on the trank to match. If you are using the patterns from this book, you can select the thumb from a larger or smaller size and trace its corresponding thumb hole onto your personal pattern.

Finally, make sure that you are accounting for your intended construction and materials. If you will be turning the seam allowances to the inside, they will add some thickness and length on top of your hand measurement and result in a snugger fit. If you will be leaving the allowances on the outside, a whipstitch allows the seam to "spread" more than a stab stitch and gives a slightly looser fit. To adjust for these differences, use a slightly larger or smaller seam allowance or go up or down a size on the base pattern (especially if you fall between sizes.)

For a stable knit fabric or a very thin, soft leather with some give, you may be able to make the glove to your exact hand measurements for a very sleek fit. With four-way stretch knits, the glove may come up smaller than your actual measurements, but not so small that it is uncomfortably tight—consider going up a size if the pattern measures less than 90% of your hand measurement. For heavier, stiffer leathers, you may want a little extra for *ease* (the term for any excess material beyond the body measurements) to ensure that you will have enough room for comfortable movement.

# WORKING WITH GLOVE PATTERNS

Once your pattern is adjusted to fit, the next challenge is cutting everything out. Professional glove makers use metal dies, like big hand-shaped cookie cutters, to punch out perfectly identical pieces. If you're looking to duplicate that mechanically perfect cut, a digital cutting machine might be a good approximation. That said, cutting by hand is just as good if you use sharp tools and work carefully. A good pair of fabric shears will do the

job along with a small pair of embroidery or trimming scissors for fine details. Or you may prefer to use a craft knife with replaceable blades and a self-healing cutting mat.

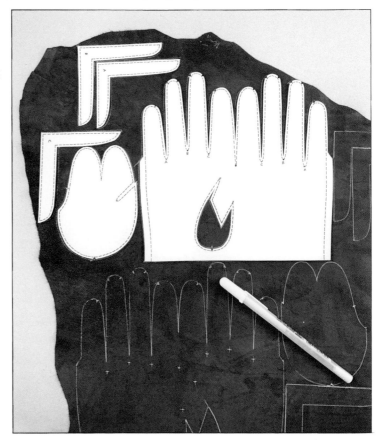

To cut and mark as accurately as possible, make a copy of the pattern on heavy paper or cardstock. Cut out the thumb opening, clip a small V into the seam allowance for each notch, and use a pushpin or awl to punch small holes for all interior markings, like the finger forks and corners of the thumb gusset.

To use the cardstock pattern, use a pen or sharp pencil to trace around the pattern directly onto the back side of your material (a silver gel pen is the leatherworker's go-to marking implement), and transfer all the notches and dots. After removing the pattern, I like to draw a small X through each dot to make it more visible.

Cut out the pieces just inside the outlines so that they end up the same size as the original pattern pieces instead of slightly larger. In some places, the stitching lines are so close together that the seam allowances merge, but you should still cut all the way to the dot. Make sure to keep the right and left pieces separate to avoid confusion. You may want to clip a label or the pattern piece to each pair of fourchettes to keep them organized as you work.

As you sew gloves together, make sure that you're using the correct seam allowance at all times. Otherwise, your seams will not match, especially where opposite curves join, like a thumb and thumb opening. The patterns included with this book have both cutting and stitching lines, so always check before you stitch.

# SIMPLIFIED GLOVE PATTERNS

One popular method for making gloves is to take the pattern directly from a hand tracing, with the thumb sticking out to the side like the hand turkey drawings you may have done in grade school. You may notice, though, that the corresponding hand position isn't actually comfortable to hold for long. In a more natural resting posture, the thumb is angled more toward the inside, which means that when you're actually wearing it, a turkey-style glove will be tight in the back and wrinkled across the palm.

Additionally, the amount of fabric it takes to go around your whole hand is not enough to wrap all the way around each finger, especially once you include seam allowances. A very stretchy fabric can make up the difference, but the tension of the stretched fabric will be uneven between the hand and fingers, and this can cause drag lines or uncomfortable tight spots across the base of each finger.

The following examples show turkey, gussetless, and fully gusseted gloves made in the same fabric to demonstrate the differences in fit. The turkey version has the fewest seams, but the thumb position creates ripples across the palm when the hand is in a natural resting posture. Splaying the fingers to create more room for seam allowances also means that each finger will be on a different grain of the fabric, which can cause unpredictable fit problems—especially if the stretch on the lengthwise and crosswise grains is different.

Adding a thumb seam, as described in Simplified Stretch Gloves (page 54), allows for more even distribution of tension, which creates a much smoother fit across the palm. However, there are still strain lines at the tightest point across the base of the fingers, and the grain problems remain.

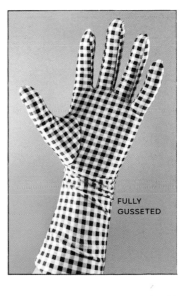

A fully gusseted glove, as described in Standard Knit Gloves (page 58), makes it possible for all the fingers to remain on the same grain, as you can see from the direction of the plaid. It will be somewhat bulkier due to the additional seams, but it is suitable for a much wider variety of fabrics, and will be more comfortable overall without the odd tight spots.

# Simplified Stretch Gloves

Although it's technically a bit of a cheat, the simplicity of a gussetless glove pattern can be very appealing in a crunch. This project aims for a compromise with gusset-free fingers but a separate thumb to provide a slightly more comfortable and anatomically correct fit. Still, you'll want to look for very soft, very stretchy fabrics that won't be uncomfortable in the tight spots.

## MATERIALS

½ yard (46cm) spandex fabric with 100% stretch in both directions

A piece of tracing paper large enough to fit your whole hand twice

A machine that does a straight stretch stitch—either a triple straight stitch or a lightning bolt stitch. (Alternatively, you can do a very small backstitch by hand.)

Printed Thumb Pattern pieces

### Thumb Pattern

To access the Thumb Pattern piece through the QR code at right, open the camera app on your phone, aim the camera at the QR code, and click the link that pops up on the screen.

To access the pattern through the tiny url, type the web address provided into your browser window. *tinyurl.com/11509-pattern2-download*

## CREATING THE PATTERN

Fold the tracing paper in half. Place your nondominant hand on the paper, with index finger and forearm aligned along the crease, fingers gently spread, and thumb sticking out past the fold. Trace around your hand and mark the top and bottom of your thumb where it crosses the fold.

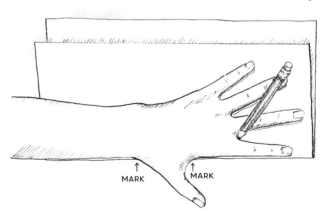

MARK     MARK

Smooth out the lines as needed to make a clean pattern. Then measure the width of each finger, knuckles, and wrist, and make sure that the number is at least 40% of the actual circumference at each corresponding spot. Lay your thumb on the thumb pattern to select a size, and trace the matching thumb opening pattern onto the palm with the reference line placed along the fold, using your top and bottom marks to guide placement.

To extend the pattern up your arm, measure your forearm, elbow, and bicep to make sure the half pattern equals about 45% of these measurements at the appropriate points, correcting the line as needed. Make sure that the line makes a smooth curve and meets the hem at a right angle.

The thumb pattern has a seam allowance indicated; you do not need to add seam allowances to the rest of the pattern as it will be cut out roughly and then trimmed after stitching.

## CUTTING

Trace the pattern onto the folded fabric with a soft pencil or gel pen, making sure that the greatest stretch goes around the hand and the lengthwise fold is aligned with the grain. Flip the pattern to trace the other hand. The line you've drawn is your actual stitching line, so when you cut it out make sure to leave at least ¼″ (6mm) of additional seam allowance all the way around. You do not need to cut around the fingers at this point. Make sure you cut the thumb opening in only the top layer. Mark the fold line so that you can accurately refold after inserting the thumb. Trace and cut 2 mirrored thumb pieces from the scraps, again making sure that the greatest stretch goes around the thumb.

## CONSTRUCTION

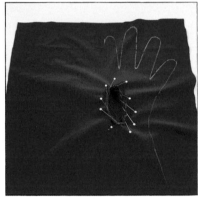

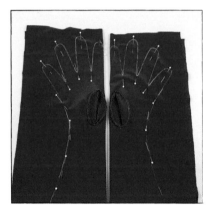

**1.** Fold the thumb in half on the dotted line and sew from the base out to the tip using a stretch stitch. Stretch stitches do not typically need backstitching to anchor the ends, but you can leave long thread tails to tie off for extra security.

**2.** Turn the thumb right side out and line it up with the thumb opening, matching the notches with right sides together. Place pins at each notch first, catching a very small bite of fabric that crosses the seam line on both sides for more precision, then add a few additional pins spaced around the opening. You will need to stretch the palm side slightly to make the lengths match up.

**3.** Stitch around the opening with the inside of the thumb facing up and the palm piece against the machine bed. Fold the trank in half and pin or baste each fingertip and fork to ensure the layers are smooth and without puckers.

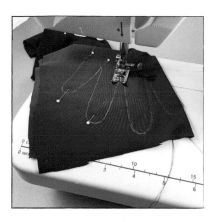

**4.** Stitch all the way around the outline using a stretch stitch. Remove the pins before you reach them so they don't distort the stitching line. When making the small pivots around the fingertips, make sure to turn at the correct point in the stitch cycle so that the forward and backward stitches all land on the line. (If you pivot and then the next stitch is a backward one, it will end up sticking out at an angle.) Use a stiletto if necessary to assist the feed and prevent it from shifting or bunching. When stitching the forks between the fingers, make one stitch straight across the bottom so you have room to cut the fingers apart later.

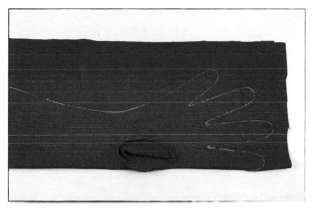

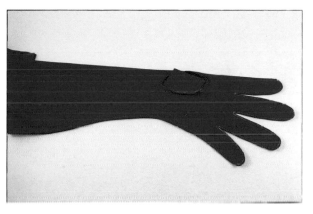

**5.** If your seams are a little wavy after stitching, you can restore them with steam. Don't touch the iron directly to the project; it's not necessary and may damage the stretch fibers.

**6.** Use sharp fabric scissors to trim very close to the stitching line. Make sure to get all the way into the corner at the forks or you will get puckers when you turn the gloves right side out.

**7.** Turn the gloves right side out and try them on. If you need to shorten any of the fingers, you can restitch the tips and trim away the excess. With a very stretchy fabric, you can sometimes reduce wrinkles across the base of the fingers by increasing the lengthwise tension. Finish by folding the hem edge down ½" (1.3cm) and securing with a zigzag or three-step zigzag stitch.

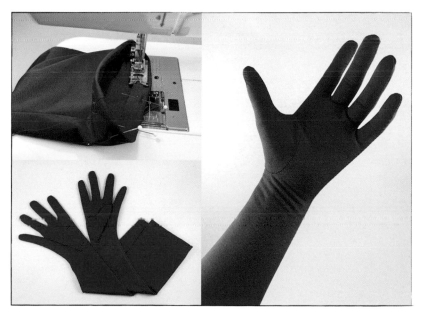

# Standard Knit Gloves

If glove making has an easy mode, it's when you use stable knit fabrics. This fabric category includes many double knits such as interlock and ponte knit, as well as scuba, jacquard knit, and some faux suedes and leathers. These materials stretch enough to ensure a comfortable and forgiving fit, but they also hold their shape when sewn and are less likely to creep, ripple, or cause skipped stitches. In some cases, you can even sew them with a straight stitch instead of with a stretch stitch, which can save a lot of time and makes it easier to unpick them if you go astray. Just make sure to test thoroughly, since taking the time to do a stretch stitch may be a lot easier than trying to repair popped seams after the fact.

Although this is a fully gusseted design, it's intended for knit fabrics with at least a small amount of stretch. At a minimum, make sure that a length of your chosen fabric equal to the narrowest measurement of the wrist has enough give to comfortably slip your hand through. This example was done in satin spandex, which has a significant amount of stretch in the lengthwise direction but almost none across, so it was cut on the cross grain so the stretch goes around the hand where it will do the most good.

## MATERIALS

¼ yard (23cm) stable knit fabric

Matching thread

Printed Standard Knit Glove Pattern pieces

### Standard Knit Glove Pattern

To access the Standard Knit Glove Pattern pieces through the QR code at right, open the camera app on your phone, aim the camera at the QR code, and click the link that pops up on the screen.

To access the pattern through the tiny url, type the web address provided into your browser window. *tinyurl.com/11509-pattern3-download*

## PATTERN AND CUTTING

Position the pieces so that the greatest stretch goes around the hand/arm, and cut 2 each of the trank, thumb, and fourchettes A, B, and C. Make sure to flip the pattern before cutting the second set so you end up with a right and a left.

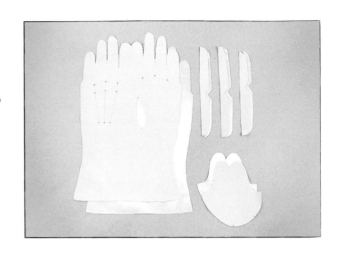

## CONSTRUCTION

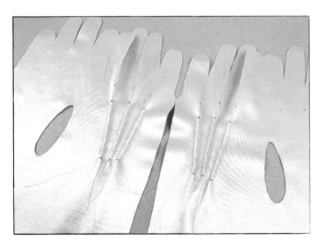

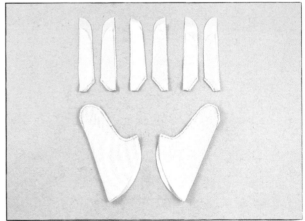

**1.** The points are optional, but they add some character and give a slightly snugger fit across the back of the hand. First, transfer your marks to the front of the fabric by basting along the line and across each end. With the right side out, fold the trank along each line in turn and stitch $1/16''$ (1.5mm) from the fold. Do not backstitch, but leave thread tails on both ends. After stitching, pull the tails to the back, knot them off, and bury the ends inside the pintuck with a hand needle.

**2.** Fold the thumb in half right sides together and stitch the side seam from the base up to the tip. Use a straight stitch or a triple straight stitch depending on how stretchy the fabric is. Stitch the darts in the fourchettes.

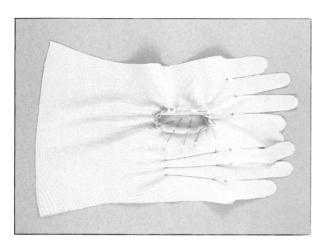
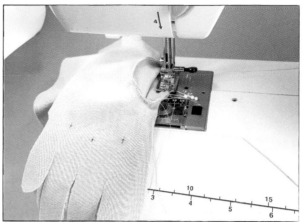

**3.** Turn the thumb right side out and line it up with the thumb opening in the trank, right sides together. Pin at the notches first to ensure they will match, then at intervals around the rest of the opening. Stitch.

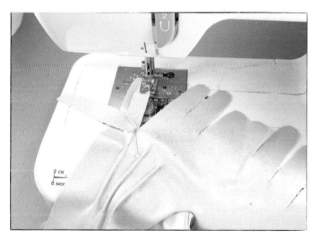
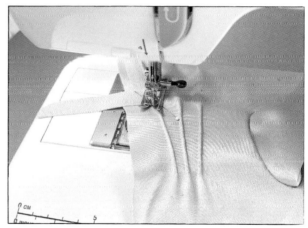

**4.** Cut the fingers apart down to about ⅛″ (3mm) from the dot. Align the first straight edge of fourchette A with the gap between the little and ring fingers on the back of the hand. Use a pin to line up the start of the seam so that the fourchette follows the slight curve of the fingertip. Place a second pin at the base of the V, flattening the seam allowance at the point of the dart and taking a very small bite of fabric that passes exactly through the dot. Grip the threads firmly as you start the seam, and use them to assist the feed until you're far enough that the feed dogs have something to grab.

**5.** Stitch down to the fork and stop with the needle down. Leave the pin in place, but walk the machine forward by hand if necessary to avoid hitting it.

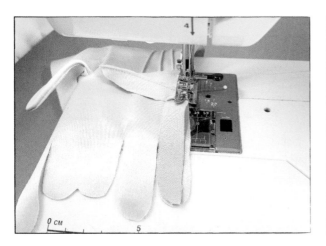

**6.** Lift the foot and use the pin as a lever to pivot the next straight edge to align with the next finger, shifting the bulk of the trank out of the way underneath.

**7.** Lower the foot and stitch up to the next fingertip dot, remembering to make the slight curve again at the end.

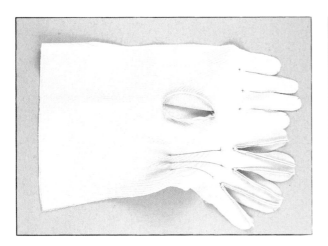

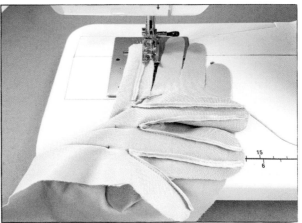

**8.** Insert the remaining two fourchettes in the back of the hand the same way. Clip the seam allowances down to the dot to prevent puckering at the point, and press the seam allowances open if your fabric permits.

**9.** Fold the trank in half to align the side seam and fingers. Start at the top of fourchette A and stitch again with the fourchette side up.

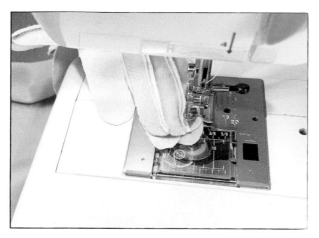

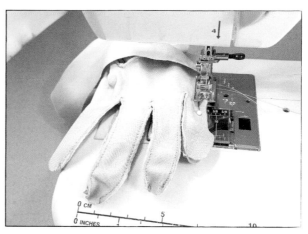

**10.** The pivot will be easier on this side because both corners are concave, but it's still helpful to put a pin at the point for alignment. Because the finger needs to wrap around the curve of the fingertip on this side, it may appear slightly too long until the seam is almost entirely sewn. As long as you stitch accurately and don't stretch the trank or fourchette, it should even up in the end.

**11.** Stitch up the remaining fingers in the same way, and sew the side seam from thumb level out to the fingertip.

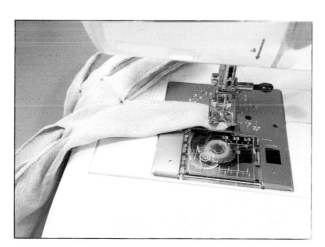

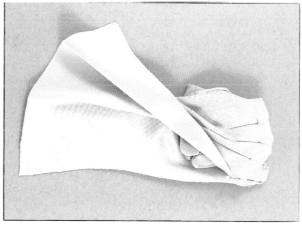

**12.** Go back and close up the fingertips. While it is sometimes possible to stitch continuously and catch both fourchettes and fingertips in a single pass, you need to be consistent about which way you're flattening the seam allowances, and it may be somewhat more difficult to keep everything aligned.

**13.** Especially when making longer gloves, it's easier to turn the fingers right side out before sewing the rest of the side seam. A bone folder or wooden tongue depressor can be helpful for neatly pressing out the fingers. As you pin and sew the seam, keep the fingers tucked out of the way between the layers so they don't get caught.

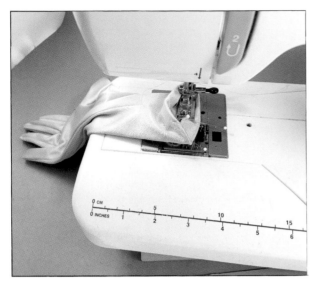 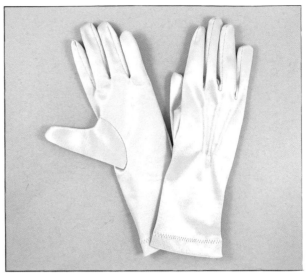

**14.** Fold the hem up and secure with topstitching or a catch stitch.

## LINED GLOVES

*To make lined gloves, you will need a thin, slippery knit fabric that stretches a bit crosswise but very little lengthwise. You may wish to cut a slightly smaller size or size up in the main glove so that the lining will fit neatly inside. The Standard Knit Glove Pattern (page 59) can also be used to line a leather glove.*

*Assemble both the main glove and the lining up to the point at which the hem would go in. Lay the outer layer and lining together with the palms facing each other and both wrong sides facing out. Tack the pieces together at each fingertip with a few hand stitches, making sure that none of the fingers are twisted and the stitches catch only the seam allowance so that they won't be visible from the outside. Turn the glove right side out.*

*To finish the glove, you can bind both outer layer and lining together; trim the lining and fold the outer layer up over it; or finish the outer layer with a binding or cording and then slipstitch the lining to it by hand.*

## INTEGRATING GLOVES INTO BODYSUITS

Bodysuits with integrated gloves create an impressive seamless look, but they have some unfortunate drawbacks in the era of ubiquitous touchscreens. Yes, your costume looks rad, but you practically need a personal assistant to pay for your purchases and answer messages for you—and undressing to the waist to wash your hands in a public restroom is a big ask.

You can solve the touchscreen problem by making the fingertips of your gloves conductive by embroidering in a little loop of conductive thread or by using one of the other various products sold for this purpose. Another option is to simply carry a stylus. Neither of these options account for fingerprint recognition technology, but they'll probably give you enough functionality to manage for the duration of a convention.

Still, it's important to be able to get out of your gloves sometimes, either for essential functions or just to alleviate the closed-in feeling that can set in over a long day in costume. So, in my opinion, any costume with integrated gloves should also have a hidden escape closure. You have two main options: You can either insert an invisible zipper from your knuckles to mid-forearm, or you can make a placket that goes across the base of your palm and is held in place by elastic. Either can be used with a simplified or gusseted stretch glove, depending on your preference and the bodysuit fabric.

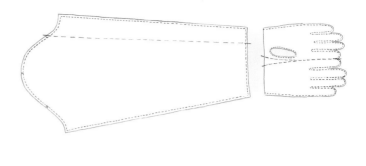

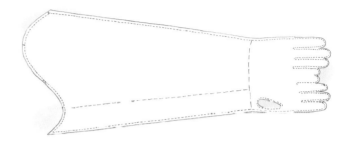

For the zipper option, you will need to reposition your sleeve seam to align with the side seam of the glove, as shown in the diagram. You can do this on either side, but many glove patterns place the seam to the outside to keep it out of the way of the thumb seam, so if you prefer the unobtrusive inside placement, you will have to move the seam on the glove piece as well and deal with a little extra bulk there. Once the seams are corrected, the entire glove trank can be merged with the sleeve piece.

When you are assembling the sleeve, construct the glove portion first, then insert the invisible zipper before sewing the rest of the sleeve seam.

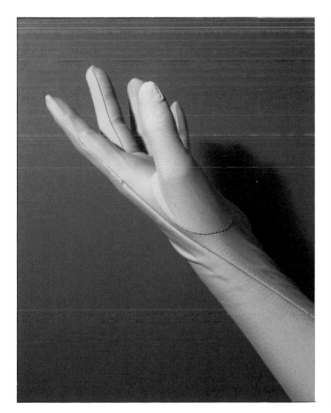

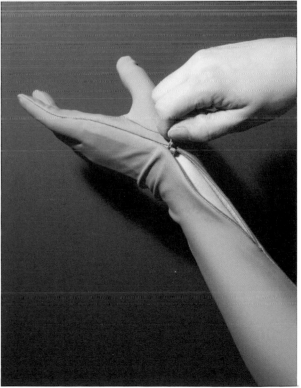

For the placket option, you don't have to change the position of the sleeve seam. The glove trank should be separated into two pieces for the front and back of the hand, and the back can be merged with the sleeve for a seamless look, but the palm should remain separate and have a hem allowance added at the lower edge. For a secure closure, make sure the sleeve fits snugly at the wrist.

Construct the glove except for the side seams, and finish the lower edge of the palm with an elastic hem. Sew the sleeve seam closed for about 3″ (7.6cm) from the wrist, then staystitch an L shape on either side of the integrated trank.

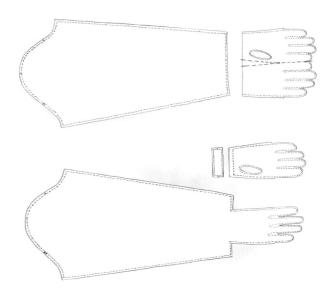

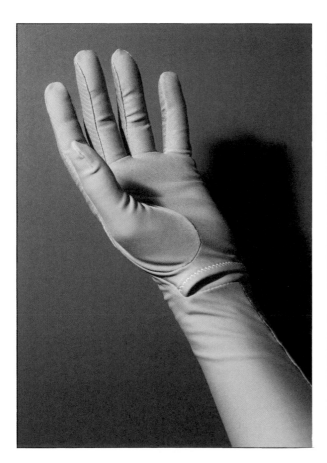

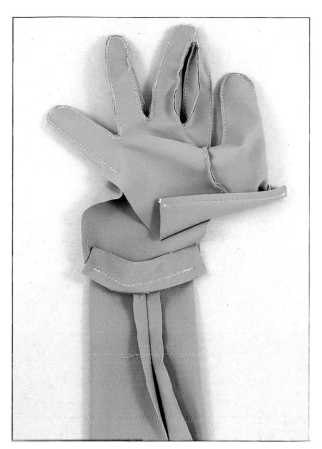

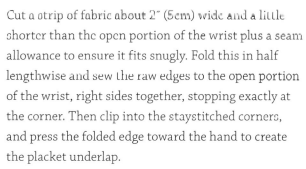

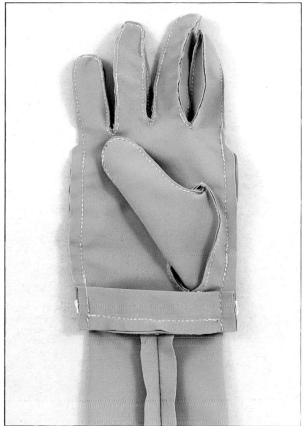

Cut a strip of fabric about 2″ (5cm) wide and a little shorter than the open portion of the wrist plus a seam allowance to ensure it fits snugly. Fold this in half lengthwise and sew the raw edges to the open portion of the wrist, right sides together, stopping exactly at the corner. Then clip into the staystitched corners, and press the folded edge toward the hand to create the placket underlap.

Finally, line up the side seams of the gloves, sandwiching the palm between the top of the hand and the underlap so the hem of the palm meets the base of the underlap. Sew the glove side seams through all three layers, again stopping exactly at the staystitched corner.

This completes the glove, so you can now sew the remaining sleeve seam and insert it in the rest of the garment.

# Leather Gloves

Fitted, nonstretch gloves are a bit of a rarity in modern fashion since stretch knit gloves are informal, inexpensive, and accommodate more hands with fewer sizes. But the classic leather-gloved look is such a staple of fantasy and historical costuming, as well as for formalwear and uniforms of various stripes, that you won't regret the time spent learning the construction and customizing your pattern to fit. This design uses the BOLTON THUMB construction, with a gusset cut into the trank pattern that joins to a slit in the thumb piece to create a sleek fit with an impressive amount of mobility.

While it is very possible to stitch a leather glove by machine, I find that stitching by hand is more pleasant and more forgiving. You can even mix and match: Finesse the tight curves and pivots by hand and then knock out the long straight seams by machine, or whatever combination suits you.

The example glove uses a whipstitch in heavy thread for visibility, with the seams turned toward the inside. However, feel free to experiment with other seaming styles as discussed in Hand Stitches (page 12). The same basic construction will work with a backstitch, which will take longer but produces a slightly tighter seam. You could also use whipstitches or stab stitches turned decoratively to the outside or construct part or all of the glove with lapped (pique) seams to reduce bulk from thicker leathers. No matter which type of seam you use, make sure that the stitching passes exactly through the stitching line marked on the pattern to ensure that the pieces match up properly.

## MATERIALS

*2 square feet (.19 square meters) of very lightweight glove leather (main color)*

*2 yards (1.9m) of ¾" (2cm) strips contrast leather or fabric*

*2 yards (1.9m) of 1/16" (1.5mm) piping cord or satin rattail cord, or substitute 2 yards (1.9m) premade piping trim.*

*Contrast scraps for bow*

*2 size #3 hook and eyes*

*Water-based leather glue*

*Printed Leather Glove Pattern pieces*

### Leather Glove Pattern

To access the Leather Glove Pattern pieces through the QR code at right, open the camera app on your phone, aim the camera at the QR code, and click the link that pops up on the screen.

To access the pattern through the tiny url, type the web address provided into your browser window. *tinyurl.com/11509-pattern4-download*

## PATTERN AND CUTTING

Cut 2 each of the trank, thumb, and fourchettes A, B, and C. Make sure to cut all the way to the dots at the finger forks, corners of the thumb opening, and thumb slash. Make sure to flip the pattern before cutting the second set so you end up with a right and a left. Cut 4 of the cuff to allow for a lining; the cuff is symmetrical so it does not need to be flipped.

## CONSTRUCTION

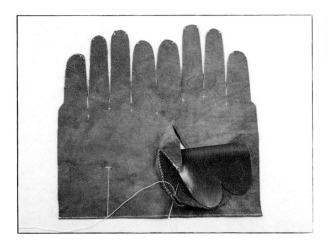

**1.** Beginning with the trank and thumb piece, start your thread at point *a* on the trank (at the lowermost point of the thumb gusset), which joins to point *a* on the thumb piece (at the notch on the side opposite the slash). Stitch up the side of the gusset to the dot (point *b*). Continue around the lower curve of the thumb, easing it into the opening so that the lower notches align.

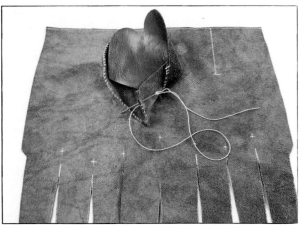

**2.** Stitch back up the other side of the thumb, around the acute corner at point *c*, and up to point *d*, joining the slash in the thumb piece to the other side of the thumb gusset.

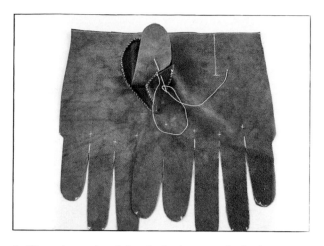

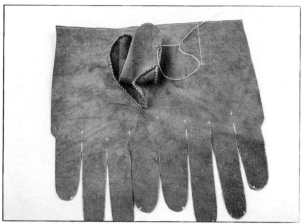

**3.** The other side of the slash aligns with the bottom of the gusset, bringing you back to the starting point at *a*. Try the thumb on to see if the tip needs to be trimmed down before you finish it.

**4.** Close up the end of the thumb. When you reach the fold line, knot your thread and weave it back through the last few stitches to secure.

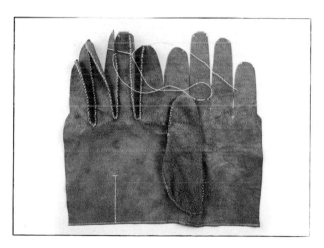

**5.** Stitch the flat outside edges of the fourchettes between the fingers on the back of the hand, matching fourchette A to notch A, fourchette B to notch B, and C to C. If the finger lengths don't match, make sure you're using the pieces for the correct hand. If you have trouble keeping the gusset centered in the notch as you stitch, try starting at the point of the V and stitching toward the fingertips on both sides.

**6.** Stitch the inside of the fourchettes (with curved fingertips) into the palm of the hand, and close the fingertips. Again, while it's safer to start at the center of each V and work outward, it's possible—and very satisfying—to start at the folded side of the pointer finger and close everything up in one continuous seam.

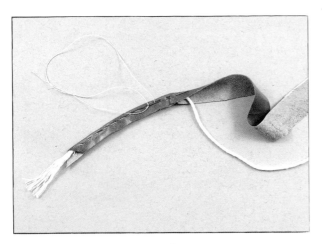

**7.** If you are not using premade piping, wrap your piping material around the cord and secure it with a basting stitch.

**8.** Cut the vent on the back of the hand open and turn the glove right side out. Stitch in a short piece of piping as a continuous loop, knotting off ¼″ (6mm) from the cut edge so the seam allowances are free.

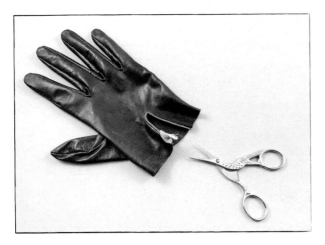

**9.** Clip into the seam allowance around the corner at the top of the vent so it will lie flat when you turn the seam allowances to the inside. Secure the seam allowances with a light coat of leather glue. Pull out the ends of the piping cord and trim away ¼″ (6mm) to reduce bulk in the seam allowance. Tuck the ends of the cording in so the cord tapers to nothing at the seam.

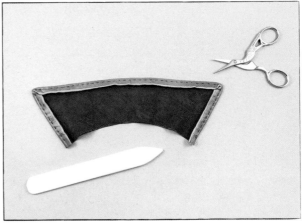

**10.** Stitch piping along the free edge of the cuff, again clearing the seam allowances and tapering the cord to nothing at the wrist seam. Fold the allowances to the inside. Lightly hammer the corners to flatten, or trim out some of the excess if the layers seem too bulky.

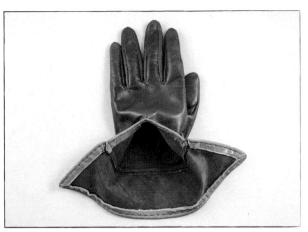

**11.** Line up the remaining raw edge of the cuff with the wrist edge of the glove, right sides together, and stitch.

**12.** If adding a full lining—see Lined Gloves (page 64)—press the seam open and lay the hand lining across it. Otherwise, grade the seam allowances and press them toward the cuff.

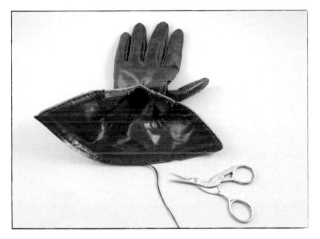

**13.** Brush the entire inside of the cuff with a light coat of water-based leather glue. Smooth the cuff lining into place, maintaining the curve and allowing any excess to hang over the edges. Edgestitch or stitch in the ditch next to the piping around the outside edge of the cuff, and whipstitch the inside edge to the seam allowances around the wrist. Trim the excess lining close to the stitching.

**14.** To make a "ribbon" from your accent leather or fabric, cut a 4″ × 12″ (10cm × 30.5cm) strip, fold in half lengthwise, and stitch with a ¼″ (6mm) seam allowance, leaving a 2″ (5cm) gap in the center to turn it out. Open and flatten the seam allowance at the center of the ribbon, then stitch across both ends at an angle.

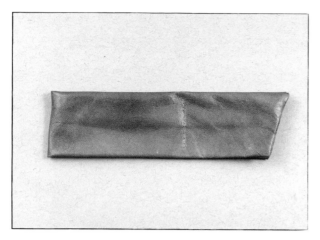

**15.** Turn and stitch closed. (If the leather is too thick to turn out nicely but still soft enough to make a nice bow, you can either use a single-layer strip of any width, or edgestitch two layers together with no seam allowance.)

**16.** Fold the ribbon in half and stitch across the double layer 3½″ (8.9cm) from the fold.

**17.** Flatten the loop and pinch the middle to make a bow shape.

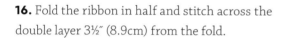

**18.** Wrap thread around it several times to secure it.

**19.** Cover the thread with a scrap of leather, secured with a few hand stitches, to make the "knot."

**20.** Sew the hook and eye in at the wrist seam so that the edges just meet when closed. Stitch the bow on top of the hook side of the opening.

## FINGERLESS GLOVES

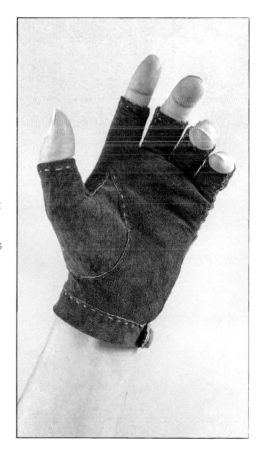

Fingerless gloves might keep less of your hand warm, but they use nearly all of the same construction techniques as a full glove. You can begin with the Standard Knit Glove Pattern (page 59) or Leather Glove Pattern (page 69), depending on your intended material, but avoid the hand turkey style as the fit issues will be exaggerated by the lack of tension through the fingers.

Determine where you would like the fingers to end—around the first knuckle is probably the most common style—and allow about ¼″ (6mm) beyond that for a hem. You may also want slightly more room in the fingers so that there's room for the hem and the gloves are easier to get on and off. Remove any taper from the pattern so that the only space between fingers is the seam allowance, and round up if you're between sizes.

Construct the gloves according to the instructions for the pattern. When you would typically close up the fingertips, instead fold the edge down and sew a single-fold hem. For leather gloves, you should also glue down the raw edge so the gloves go on smoothly; for knits, you can simply trim close to the stitching or choose a stitch that goes over the edge.

# HAND AND ARM ARMOR

## ARMOR MATERIALS

With actual protection in battle off the priority list, costume armor can be made out of almost anything. EVA foam is one of the most popular options, followed by thermoplastics, leather, industrial felt, and others. Each has advantages and drawbacks, but in most cases, the choice comes down to what you prefer to work with.

EVA foam is popular because it is inexpensive, lightweight, and flexible, making it one of the most comfortable types of armor to wear. Cut it with a craft knife or razor blade and shape it with heat and sanding and it can look astonishingly convincing once it's sealed and painted. The main disadvantages are the mess and toxicity during nearly every step of the process. Foam releases fumes when heated, produces vast clouds of noxious dust when sculpted by sanding, and is most effectively glued with contact cement, which contains a variety of unfriendly solvents. As a result, this material is best suited for those with a dedicated, well-ventilated workspace.

Thermoplastics such as Worbla are thin, durable, contain their own adhesive, and, after activating with heat, can be shaped over a substrate or sculpted like clay (which means that scraps are reusable, reducing waste). The resulting armor is hard and sturdy but still slightly flexible, depending on the thickness, and can hold an impressive amount of detail. The main drawback is the cost of the material, and the resulting armor is stiff and heavy compared with other options, so it may be less comfortable to wear.

Veg-tan leather is generally too stiff for clothing, but it can be carved, stamped, sewn, wet molded, and riveted into all kinds of armor pieces. It is one of the most durable options for costume armor, given that it is one of the few materials also used for real armor, and it's more flexible and breathable than some alternatives. It hardens somewhat when wet shaped and dyed, and various treatments exist for hardening it still further. That said, it is more expensive and less forgiving than some of the other options.

Industrial felt is most commonly found in 3mm or 5mm thickness and is made from wool, polyester, or acrylic fibers. It makes a soft but structural base that's easy to sew and cover with other materials, as in the Simple Bracer project (page 78). However, it's typically not very armor-like on its own.

Fosshape is like a sewable hybrid of thermoplastic and fabric. It starts out lofty and flexible, like thick felt or batting, but hardens when heated and compressed. You can shape it by hand with steam, flatten it with an iron, or heat press it to make a thin, tough fiberboard. It makes a sturdy, lightweight understructure that holds its shape well, but it usually needs to be covered with something to make a smooth surface. It also shrinks unpredictably during hardening, so it's best to leave a little extra and then trim after shaping.

# Simple Bracer

In addition to being one of the simplest and most versatile types of armwear you can add to a costume, bracers are an excellent first armor project. They don't take much material, so they're great for experimenting with expensive supplies like leather or thermoplastics. On top of that, the one-piece design is a perfect foundation for embellishment. This version uses quilting details and prong-back studs, but you could also add detail with appliqué, rivets, purchased trims, a painted design, or anything else you can think of.

## MATERIALS

*18" (46cm) square of 2–3mm industrial felt or 1 yard (91cm) craft interfacing*

*½ yard (46cm) outer decorative fabric or 2 square feet (.19 square meters) of soft leather plus additional 2" (5cm) strips for binding*

*½ yard (46cm) faux suede or 2 square feet (.19 square meters) of suede for lining*

*Tracing wheel and tracing paper*

*Leather glue to hold layers together for quilting (substitute fusible web if using all heat-safe fabrics)*

*20 size 00 grommets and setter*

*3 yards (2.7m) leather cording, ribbon, or shoelace*

## CREATING THE PATTERN

To decide how long you would like the bracer to be, lay a ruler on your forearm and measure up from the wrist. Mark the top edge position with a washable marker or dot of tape. While wearing whatever garments you intend to wear under the bracer, measure around your wrist and around your forearm at the top mark.

On a piece of paper, draw a rectangle as long as your forearm measurement and as wide as your wrist measurement. Fold the rectangle in half lengthwise, then in half again, and cut along your crease lines so the piece is split into equal quarters. At one end, spread the quarter segments until the total width matches your upper forearm measurement. Tape them down on a piece of paper and connect the segments into smooth curves at the top and bottom. You now have a pattern for a basic conical shape that can be used to develop the final bracer pattern.

To design the bracer, first decide how it will be fastened and finished. Trim away roughly ½" (1.3cm) from each straight edge to create a gap for lacing up the inside or a little more if you will close it with straps and buckles. Redraw the top and bottom edges into whatever shapes you please, and round off the corners so you can finish them with a smooth binding all the way around. (Other options include piping, an appliquéd border in a nonfraying material, or adding an allowance for a simple hem.)

Draw in your desired details. I opted for a slightly graduated diamond quilting pattern with prong-back studs, but you could also add detail with appliqué, paint, or trim. Remember that the binding will take up about ¼" (6mm) of space all the way around the edge.

## CUTTING

Cut 2 of the bracer base from felt or interfacing, 2 from the lining material, and 2 from the outer fabric. Leave a little excess material around the edges so that you can adjust if anything shifts during quilting. If the shape you've drawn is asymmetrical, remember to flip the pattern to get a left and a right. Use a tracing wheel to transfer your quilting design to the leather face.

Cut 2 of the 2″ (5cm) binding strips long enough to go all the way around each bracer. If you are using leather, make sure that it is thin and flexible enough to fold over, or pick a binding leather that complements your main leather. If you are using fabric, the binding should be cut on the bias.

## CONSTRUCTION

**1.** Apply a light coat of leather glue to the back of the leather piece and let it get a little viscous before applying the felt so it doesn't soak in and lose its grip. Compress with a book or heavy board while it dries. If you are using fabric instead of leather, you can substitute fusible web for the glue. Quilt along the marked lines with heavy thread or a double thickness of all-purpose thread and a stitch length of about 3.5mm. If you are using leather, you may need a roller or nonstick foot to allow smooth feeding. Stop just inside the outline of your finished piece so you can knot the ends instead of trimming them off for a little extra security.

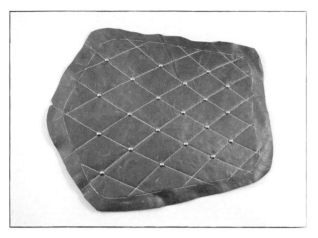

**2.** Pull the thread ends to the back side and knot off. Apply prong-back studs to the intersections of the quilting lines using a hand press, mallet and die, or pliers to bend the prongs into place. You want to apply enough pressure to grip the material firmly, but not so much that the studs punch through the surface. If you wish, you can substitute glue on or rivet back studs.

**3.** Use your original pattern as a guide to trim the excess material around the edges.

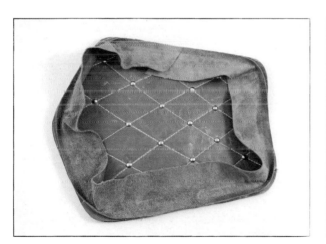

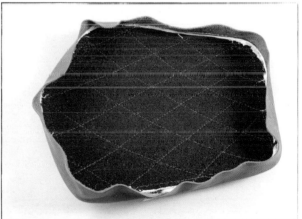

**4.** Align the binding with the cut edge, right sides together. If you are using a fabric binding, fold the raw end in ¼″ (6mm) before you stitch so that it will be tucked inside the completed binding. Stitch about ¼″ (6mm) from the edge all the way around, easing the binding slightly around the curves. When you get back to the start, overlap the end and cut off the excess.

**5.** Wrap the binding around to the underside. If you are using fabric, press to get a nice crisp edge. For leather, add a little glue close to the bracer edge to help hold the fold in place.

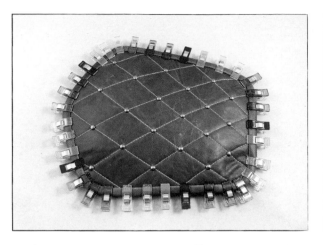

**6.** Flatten the edge with a soft mallet, or crease with a bone folder or roller, and secure with fabric clips until dry. Be especially firm around the corners so that you won't get hung up on them when stitching.

**7.** Trim the excess so that the curves lie as flat as possible, leaving about ⅛″ (3mm) to cover the stitching.

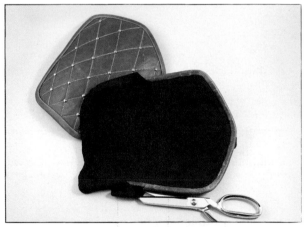

**8.** Apply fabric glue to the inside of your lining material and lay it glue side up over an arm form or another cylindrical object. Smooth the bracer over the lining, making sure that the binding is nicely tucked in and the lining covers the raw edges all the way around. Wrap scrap fabric around the bracer to hold it in the curved shape until the glue is dry.

**9.** Stitch in the ditch right next to the fold of the binding, making sure to catch the binding and lining layers underneath. Trim the lining close to the stitching.

**10.** Mark and punch holes on each side for the laces. Two-part grommets are sturdier than one-part eyelets, but since a bracer doesn't need to be laced very tight, you can use whatever is readily available. I prefer a mallet and die–style grommet setter over the pliers type, as you can apply more force with less effort. Lace the bracer from the top, so that the ties are at the narrowest point and the bracer will be easier to get into.

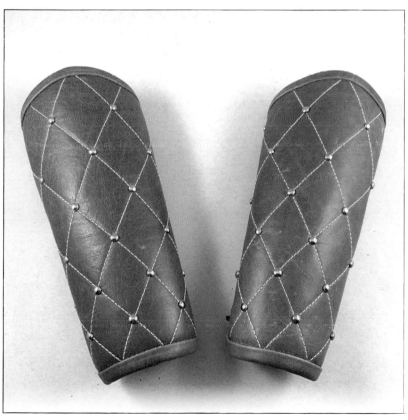

# Segmented Vambrace

When you are creating armor that extends past the elbow, there's a tricky balance of maintaining mobility while making sure everything stays put. Simply strapping pieces around your upper arm is not a great bet—they're either too tight when you flex or they slide down when you relax, and there's nothing to stop them from rotating around your arm when you least want them to. If the design permits, you can attach the armor to your clothing, but that's not always possible either—and it's often just not as satisfying as using functional straps.

The alternative is to anchor the upper arm to another piece of armor in a way that adds stability without compromising mobility. Unlike the shoulder, the elbow is a very simple joint that moves on a single axis. That means you can accommodate a good range of motion with a single, well-placed pivot, as this vambrace does.

The upper arm, elbow, and lower arm pieces in this vambrace all connect with a single Chicago screw pivot. That means each piece can be constructed and finished individually, then joined at the end. The pieces can also be disassembled for repair or transport. The pivot keeps all three pieces aligned during wear but shouldn't interfere with movement as long as it's positioned correctly. Hidden elastic in the straps adds a little extra flex to keep everything snug as your muscles change shape with movement.

The example piece is made from Worbla backed with cardstock, but I've also made it in veg-tan leather. The pattern should work equally well in Fosshape or foam, so long as you adjust the assembly method to match the medium.

## MATERIALS

*Medium-sized roll of Worbla or similar thermoplastic*

*6 letter-sized sheets of cardstock*

*2 square feet (.19 square meters) of garment leather, faux leather, or suede for straps*

*¼ yard (23cm) faux suede or felt for lining*

*6 buckles ⅝" (1.6cm)*

*1 yard (91cm) heavy-duty elastic ⅝" (1.6cm)*

*2 Chicago screws ⅜" (1cm)*

*Water-based leather glue*

*Hot glue*

*Primer (I prefer acrylic gesso) and paint*

*Arm form (see Making an Arm Form, page 32)*

*Heat gun*

*Silicone baking mat or other nonstick heat-resistant surface*

*Sculpting tools*

*Hole punches in 3mm and 5mm sizes*

*Printed Vambrace Pattern pieces*

## PATTERN AND CUTTING

To adjust the pattern for length and width, cut along the indicated lines and overlap or add paper as needed. Make a paper mock-up to check your work—the forearm section should extend from your wrist to the middle of your elbow joint and both the lower and upper arm pieces should wrap about three-quarters of the way around your arm, leaving room for straps and buckles. After adjusting, redraw the lines so that they're smooth.

Cut 2 each of the 3 forearm pieces, elbow piece, and 3 upper arm pieces from cardstock, remembering to flip the pieces to get a right and a left. To cut the strap slots neatly, use the 3mm hole punch to cut out each end of the slot, and then slice between them with a craft knife. Use the 5mm hole punch to cut the pivot holes for the Chicago screws.

Roughly cut the Worbla to be about ½″ (1.3cm) larger than the cardstock pieces all the way around. Measure your arm at the wrist, just below the elbow and around the bicep, double each measurement, and add 1½″ (3.8cm). For each length, cut 2 strips of garment leather ⅝″ (1.6cm). Cut 6 pieces of elastic 2½″ (6.4cm).

# CONSTRUCTION

**1.** Fold each cardstock piece along the center dashed and dotted line and then flatten again. You will use this crease to add shape later, and it will be more difficult to get a clean fold after applying the plastic.

**2.** One by one, heat the thermoplastic pieces on the nonstick work surface until sticky. Press the cardstock pieces down on top and rub all over with your thumbnail or a tool to make sure they fully adhere. On the outer edges of the forearm and upper arm base pieces, fold the thermoplastic around the edges of the cardstock. Reheat as needed to keep the material soft and workable. Use sculpting tools to squish the excess at the corners out into an even layer and to sculpt a nice crisp edge. Trim away the excess from edges that will be joined to other pieces so that the end seam will be less chunky. (If you would like the seam to be flatter still, you can glue the card pieces together and then drape a single sheet of thermoplastic over the whole piece.) Use a sculpting tool to clear the plastic from the strap slots.

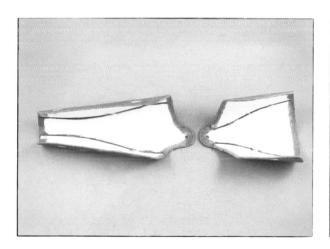

**3.** Heat both sides of each seam on the lower and upper arm pieces and press together firmly to join. Use a sculpting tool to shape the edge of the seam so that it makes an attractive detail. Shape the pieces into a curve around your arm or foil-wrapped arm form.

**4.** Cut felt or faux suede slightly larger than the pieces and glue it in to cover the cardstock on the inside. Hot glue is best for this as it will not warp the cardstock, but use a light touch as large blobs can hold enough heat to soften the thermoplastic. Trim the lining just inside the edges of the armor and slice the strap slots open with a craft knife.

**5.** Fold each strap in half and mark the center, then punch two holes on either side of the center point and snip between them to make an oval-shaped opening. Slide the buckle onto the strap and apply glue to about 2″ (5cm) of the strap next to the buckle, plus 3½″ (8.9cm) of the strap at one end. Fold the strap back on itself and secure the glued areas with clips until dry.

**6.** Use the tab template to mark and punch three holes at the free end of the strap and trim it into a point. Thread the strap through the slots on the vambrace pieces so that the buckle sits right at the slot and the strap follows the curve of the armor. Mark the vambrace center line on the strap.

**7.** Cut straight across the strap at the mark and apply glue to both sides of the unglued section. Lay a piece of elastic between the leather layers, overlapping ½″ (1.3cm) on each side so that a 1½″ (3.8cm) span of elastic connects the two halves of the strap. Secure with clips again until dry. Stitch by hand or machine all the way around the straps to secure the edges and elastic. On the machine, you will not be able to stitch all the way to the buckle, but get as close as you can and then tie off your threads.

**8.** Thread the straps through their openings in the base pieces and position them so that the elastic is centered on the center line. Stitch down the middle to secure without interfering with the stretch. (Most sewing machines can stitch through a single layer of Worbla, but if yours struggles you can substitute rivets.) Heat a small scrap of thermoplastic to cover the stitching on the outside, and use a sculpting tool to blend it smoothly into the surface.

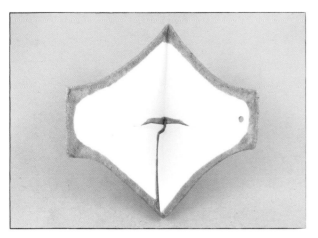

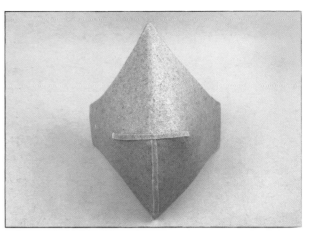

**9.** On the elbow piece, fold the thermoplastic to the inside around the edges and blend smooth with a sculpting tool. Cut along the solid lines into the three-way dart. To close the dart, bring the dotted line over to the cut edge and use the Worbla on the tab to stick it together—first the horizontal legs, then the center vertical portion. This should give you a roughly pyramidal shape with the cardstock on the inside.

**10.** Cut small strips from your thermoplastic scraps and apply them over the dart seams on the outside. Sculpt into a clean edge.

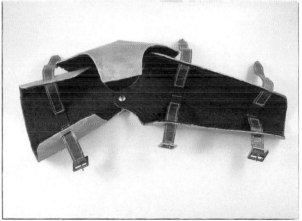

**11.** Lightly sand your pieces to help the paint adhere to the plastic. Prime with gesso or a flexible primer of your choice, then paint with liquid metallic acrylic paint and seal with acrylic varnish to help prevent the paint from rubbing off around the pivot.

**12.** When everything is dry, assemble the pieces with the Chicago screws.

# Full Gauntlet

Detailed gauntlets are one of the most challenging tasks in armoring or glove making, on the basis of organization alone. Hands are the most densely articulated and mobile parts of the body, so armoring them with rigid materials requires many, many (many) points of articulation as well. To keep track of all 30 finger armor segments in this project, each is labeled with a letter indicating the finger (Index, Middle, Ring, Pinky, and Thumb) and a number (1 for the segment closest to the knuckles, 3 for the fingertip), to which you should add Right and Left indicators as you cut them out.

Since much of the glove will be assembled after the armor is in place, it should be constructed right side out. Choose a stitch type for the prix seam that will look nice on both sides, like a stab stitch, whipstitch, or blanket stitch. The exception is the initial partial construction of the thumb and fourchettes, which can be done using whatever method you like if you don't mind mixing your seam types. I used a lapped (pique) seam for the back of the hand to keep it a little smoother under the armor.

The armor is attached with mini rivets in the example, but if you can't find them, you can simply stitch the armor to the base glove at each pivot point, using several stitches in the same spot and allowing enough slack to preserve the movement.

## Full Gauntlet Pattern

To access the Full Gauntlet Pattern pieces through the QR code at right, open the camera app on your phone, aim the camera at the QR code, and click the link that pops up on the screen.

To access the pattern through the tiny url, type the web address provided into your browser window. *tinyurl.com/11509-pattern6-download*

## MATERIALS

*2 square feet (.19 square meters) of light- to medium-weight glove leather (1 oz. or less)*

*2 square feet (.19 square meters) of 2–3 oz. (0.8–1.2mm thickness) veg-tan leather for the knuckles and finger armor*

*1 square foot (.1 square meters) of thin leather or suede for the cuff lining*

*7 dozen 4mm rivets*

*Rivet setter*

*Dot anvil*

*Mallet*

*Craft knife*

*2mm hole punch*

*Sandpaper*

*Leather dye or paint*

*Acrylic paint for weathering*

*Printed Leather Glove Pattern pieces (page 69)*

*Printed Full Gauntlet Pattern pieces*

# PATTERN AND CUTTING

Use the trank, fourchettes, and thumb from the Leather Glove Pattern (page 69), but go up one size for a looser fit to help balance out the stiffness of the armor. Where the pattern curves in at the wrist, instead extend the line straight down to make it large enough to put on without a fastener. Use the longer gauntlet cuff to match the widened trank.

The finger armor segments are sized to fit together and pivot cleanly, but you may need to adjust the length of the first and second segments to match your finger proportions. The easiest way to see what needs to be lengthened or shortened and where is to cut out and assemble a full set with heavy paper. Remember to fit the mock-up over a similar glove, as armor sized to fit a bare hand will end up too small.

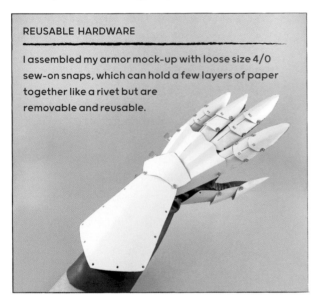

### REUSABLE HARDWARE

I assembled my armor mock-up with loose size 4/0 sew-on snaps, which can hold a few layers of paper together like a rivet but are removable and reusable.

The rivet placements for the armor are easiest to check on a fully assembled mock-up glove as well. (If you don't have one, you can do this with the partially assembled glove when you get to that step, holding the fourchettes between your fingers to keep the glove in place.) Place the middle segment of each finger first to ensure that the finger will bend in the right place, then use those marks as a guide to place the other segments. If working on your own hand is too difficult, use a similarly sized hand of a friend. Use double-sided tape to hold the armor pieces in place while you mark the positions of the holes, then copy the placements onto the pattern for your final glove.

Note that the overlapping segments are slightly wider than their underlaps to allow for movement, so the pieces will need to be curved to align the rivet holes. To adjust the length of a particular segment, cut across it perpendicular to the center line and overlap the pieces or tape in additional paper as needed. If adding width, add the same amount to all the pieces for that finger so that they will still fit together correctly.

In glove leather, cut 2 each of the trank, fourchettes, and thumb, remembering to flip the pattern pieces for a left and a right. Cut 2 cuffs in your main leather and an additional 2 in the same or thinner leather for lining.

From the veg-tan leather, cut 2 mirrored copies of the knuckles, wrist plate, cuff plate, and all 15 finger armor segments. Due to the thickness of the leather and the precision required, you will probably find it easiest to do this with a craft knife and cutting mat. Be sure to label all the segments, including whether the piece is for the right or left, and punch all rivet holes. If needed, lightly sand the edges of your pieces to clean up the cuts.

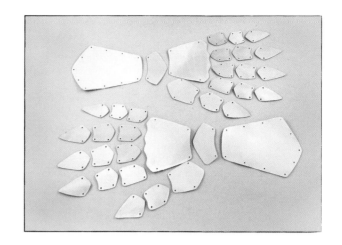

## CONSTRUCTION

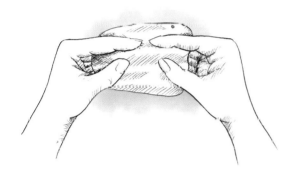

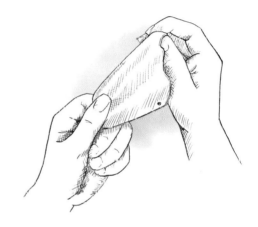

**1.** Dip the knuckle piece in a bowl of water (do not let it soak) and allow it to rest for a few minutes. Pinch between your fingers along the marked lines to create four ridges that point along the lines of your fingers.

**2.** Pinch the point that will go over each knuckle between your thumb and forefinger and use the pad of your thumb to lightly stretch it into a rounded shape.

**3.** Wet the wrist, gauntlet, and finger segments and shape them individually. The wrist and cuff plates can be shaped over an arm form (see Making an Arm Form, page 32). The wrist sits on top of the gauntlet, so it should be a slightly wider curve. If you wish to add tooled details to either, do this now and then shape the leather while it's still moist. Finger segments 1 and 2 can be wrapped around a thick marker to get the right shape; the fingertips should be hand shaped to get a cool-looking point. Apply leather dye of your choice, then wrap the pieces in strips of muslin to hold the shape while they dry.

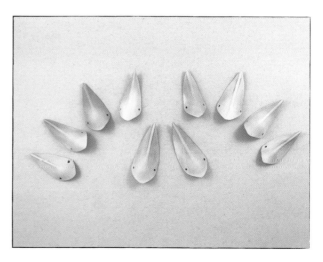

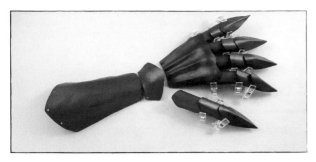

**4.** You may find that the leather curls out of shape as it dries; if so, you can lightly rewet the pieces with a brush and adjust as needed. Once the pieces are reshaped and dried, buff each piece with a rag to remove excess dye and give the leather a nice shine.

**5.** Use acrylic paint to add additional details and weathering to the segments, and paint the undersides black or another unobtrusive color in case they show during movement.

**6.** Follow the instructions for Leather Gloves (page 68) to assemble the thumb and insert the fourchettes in the back of the hand. Sew the cuff to the trank using a standard or pique seam.

**7.** Begin each finger with the pair of rivets joining the glove to segments 2 and 3.Use an awl to poke a small hole in the glove at each mark. Slide segment 1 under segment 2 and insert the rivets joining that pair, then attach the base of segment 1. Insert the rivet posts through the glove first, then the underlapping finger segment, then the overlapping segment. Usually finger pressure will secure the cap well enough to hold until you can hammer it into place. Use an appropriately sized setting tool to keep the rivet cap nicely rounded. You want to set the rivets firmly enough to hold, but not so firmly that they lock up and can't pivot.

**8.** The bottom outermost rivet on the index finger also attaches to the knuckle plate, so leave that undone until the rest of the finger segments are on. For the middle and ring fingers, place segment 1 on the finger directly and mark the rivet positions on either side. (If having rivets between your fingers seems too uncomfortable, you can instead use stitches in this first set of holes as they are unlikely to be visible.) When you reach the pinky, leave the outside set of rivets undone as they land very close to the seam and may interfere with closing up the glove. Instead move on to the knuckle, wrist, and gauntlet plates.

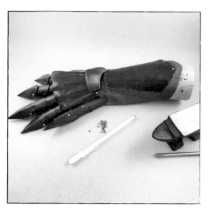

**9.** Clip the outside seam of the glove closed so you can position and rivet the knuckle and cuff plates. The wrist plate attaches on top of the cuff plate, using the pair of cuff rivets nearest the wrist seam.

**10.** Fold down the hem allowance on the cuff piece, glue in place, and lightly hammer or roll with a seam roller to get a crisp edge. Sand the lower edge slightly to help the lining stick. Glue in the lining, covering the rivet backs and the wrist seam. Allow the extra material to extend past the hem and seam edges for now, and leave about ½" (1.3cm) unglued along both sides of the side seam.

**11.** Begin to close up the fingers according to the instructions for Leather Gloves (step 5, page 71). Continue around to the tip of the pinky finger, but don't finish the side seam until the remaining pinky rivets are set.

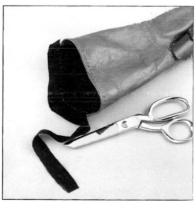

**12.** Sew a few stitches past the first rivet mark, then get out your dot anvil and set the rivet while the inside of the rivet hole is still easily accessible. Continue stitching just past the next rivet and repeat.

**13.** Close up the side seam of the glove and cuff in stages so that it's easier to lap the ends of the cuff lining across the seam on the inside and glue them down as you go. When you reach the end of the side seam, continue stitching around the hem of the cuff. Trim the hem edge of the lining close to the stitching.

**14.** Using a waxed length of regular sewing thread in an unobtrusive color, stitch the sides of each fingertip to the edges of finger plate 3 to help the armor move naturally with the fingers. Use a dab of paint to further conceal the stitches if needed.

# ABOUT THE AUTHOR

Gillian Conahan is the author of *The Hero's Closet: Sewing for Cosplay and Costuming*. A professional stage costumer and former sewing magazine editor, she relentlessly collects techniques and has stitched on everything from corsetry to mascot suits. In her personal cosplay she is an omnivorous handcraft nerd, drawing on leathercraft, thermoplastics, shoemaking, painting, weaving, and chainmail in addition to sewing and needlework.

Originally from Portland, OR, Gillian studied science writing at MIT and now lives in Brooklyn with a well-fed fabric stash. She occasionally blogs at **ALLTOMORROWSPATTERNS.COM**

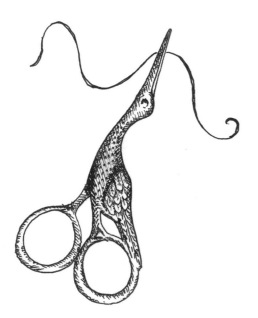